RECLAIMING THE FUTURE

RECLAIMING THE FUTURE

A PRACTICAL BLUEPRINT FOR ECONOMIC
TRANSFORMATION AND HUMAN RIGHTS

JD ROSSETTI

Copyright © 2025 by Juxtapolitico

Juxtapolitico.com

All rights reserved.

No part of this book may be reproduced in any form or by any electronic or mechanical means, including information storage and retrieval systems, without written permission from the author, except for the use of brief quotations in a book review.

This work contains fictional stories. All names and characters are fictitious. Any similarity to actual persons, living or dead, or actual events is purely coincidental.

For the builders, the dreamers, and for those who choose to act when action is needed.

*You who dare to govern with compassion,
to restore what was broken,
to reimagine what was deemed impossible.*

This is for you.

*For your courage to begin.
For your insistence that the future is not only necessary, but already underway.*

*May this book be a companion to your practice,
a provocation to your purpose, and a reminder:*

*You are the future.
Now it's your turn.
The time is yours.*

GLOSSARY OF TERMS

Glossary of Terms

1. Post-Scarcity

A social and economic condition in which technological advancement, collective resource management, and equitable policy design have made it possible to meet all basic human needs — such as food, shelter, water, education, and healthcare — without relying on artificial scarcity, price gating, or exploitative labor.

Note: Post-scarcity does *not* imply infinite resources, but rather intelligent systems that distribute resources based on sufficiency, not profitability.

2. Structural Violence

A form of harm embedded in social, economic, and

political systems that systematically disadvantages certain groups and limits access to basic needs. It is "violence" without a perpetrator — found in housing codes, loan requirements, zoning laws, healthcare access, wage gaps, and militarized borders.

3. Universal Basic Services (UBS)

A policy model that guarantees all people access to essential services — including housing, transportation, healthcare, education, and digital connectivity — provided collectively through public institutions or cooperative infrastructure, rather than through private market mechanisms or means-tested programs.

4. Trillionaire Club

A proposed global enforcement mechanism requiring any individual whose net worth exceeds $1 trillion USD to contribute directly to a Global Committee for Food and Water Security. Failure to meet measurable benchmarks results in a wealth reclamation clause through proportional taxation or asset redirection.

Subcomponents:

- Trillionaire Stewardship Index: Measures the ethical contribution of ultra-wealthy individuals toward eliminating global hunger and water scarcity.
- Trillionaire Accountability Dashboard: A public-facing tool to monitor compliance, transparency, and global impact in real time.

. . .

5. Neoliberalism

A political and economic ideology promoting deregulation, privatization, austerity, and market supremacy over public goods. It frames individual choice as the solution to systemic problems while defunding collective infrastructure and increasing inequality.

Example: Blaming a minimum wage worker for their poverty while ignoring the collapse of social safety nets and the rise of speculative finance.

6. Social Return on Investment (SROI)

An accounting methodology that measures the broader social, environmental, and economic value generated by a policy, organization, or investment — rather than focusing solely on monetary profit. SROI assigns economic value to outcomes like improved health, reduced incarceration, or increased civic engagement.

7. WELLBYs (Wellbeing-Adjusted Life-Years)

A metric used to assess the aggregate wellbeing impact of policies over time, combining lifespan and self-reported life satisfaction. Popularized in the UK and among progressive economists, WELLBYs provide a more humane alternative to GDP.

Note: One WELLBY roughly equals a one-point increase in life satisfaction sustained over one year.

8. GDP (Gross Domestic Product)

The total monetary value of goods and services produced within a country. While often used as a proxy for economic success, GDP ignores inequality, environmental degradation, unpaid labor, and quality of life. In this book, we refer to it occasionally as *Grossly Distorted Priorities*.

9. Commons-Based Governance

A model of managing shared resources — like water, energy, or digital infrastructure — through collective ownership, participatory decision-making, and long-term stewardship rather than private extraction. Inspired by Elinor Ostrom's work and practiced in many Indigenous, cooperative, and municipal contexts.

10. Doughnut Economics

A visual framework developed by economist Kate Raworth that balances human needs and planetary boundaries. The "doughnut" refers to the safe space between a social foundation (everyone's basic needs) and an ecological ceiling (Earth's limits). Policies should aim to keep us within this zone.

11. Participatory Budgeting

A democratic process in which community members directly decide how to allocate portions of public budgets. Originating in Brazil and spreading globally, this model empowers residents to fund local priorities, from park renovations to housing co-ops.

. . .

12. Securitized Scarcity

The process by which access to basic needs like water, housing, and food is deliberately limited, commodified, or weaponized through legal, financial, or military mechanisms — often for profit, political control, or artificial market preservation.

13. Defense Production Act (DPA)

A U.S. federal law allowing the government to direct industrial production in times of national emergency. While traditionally used for wartime manufacturing, this book proposes using the DPA to mobilize production for climate resilience, housing, clean energy, and public health infrastructure.

14. Circular Economy

An economic model that eliminates waste by reusing, recycling, and regenerating materials in a closed-loop system. Contrasts with the linear "take-make-dispose" economy that drives overconsumption and environmental degradation.

15. Digital Commons

Technologies, data sets, algorithms, or platforms that are owned and governed collectively — not by private companies. Examples include Wikipedia, open-source software, and community broadband networks. This book advocates for a "Civic Internet" rooted in public utility principles.

. . .

16. Shadow Parliament / Post-Scarcity Congress
A proposed coalition of civil society organizations, labor unions, climate activists, tech cooperatives, and community leaders that operates as a "people's legislature" — proposing laws, reviewing government policy, and holding public hearings in parallel to official governments.

17. Global Earth Oversight Authority (GEOA)
A visionary international institution proposed in Chapter 12 that would oversee planetary ecological health, resource stewardship, and post-capitalist trade agreements. GEOA would enforce the Trillionaire Planetary Contribution Clause and mediate climate reparations and ecological debt settlements.

18. 28TH AMENDMENT (U.S. Economic Bill of Rights 2.0)
A proposed constitutional amendment enshrining the right to basic economic security in the U.S. — including guaranteed access to food, housing, education, healthcare, and meaningful employment. Builds on FDR's 1944 Economic Bill of Rights.

19. Open-Source Governance
A form of policymaking and administrative design where laws, tools, data, and code are publicly accessible and collaboratively editable. Encourages transparency, innovation, and decentralized problem-solving.

20. Civic Tech

Technology tools that empower citizens to participate in governance — including budget simulators, legislative co-design platforms, public meeting apps, and AI tools for analyzing bills. It is the infrastructure of a living, participatory democracy.

FOREWORD

What if scarcity was a lie — and justice was a design challenge?

In an age defined by paradox — obscene wealth alongside starvation, trillion-dollar fortunes amid planetary collapse, overflowing homes while families sleep in cars — a new kind of book has arrived. Bold, actionable, and grounded in rigorous analysis, *Reclaiming the Future* dares to ask the one question most economists, politicians, and pundits avoid:

What would it actually take to build a world where every person's basic needs are guaranteed — and the planet thrives in balance?

This is not a book of wishful thinking or empty slogans. It is a full-spectrum blueprint for economic transformation, grounded in the best of modern interdisciplinary research, post-growth economics, public health equity, environmental governance, and human rights law.

Whether you're a policymaker looking for serious frameworks, a movement builder hungry for strategy, or a concerned citizen searching for hope that isn't naive, *Reclaiming the Future* offers something rare: moral clarity, legal precision, and practical pathways forward.

What You'll Find Inside:

- An unapologetic diagnosis of capitalism's structural violence — how scarcity is manufactured, inequality is systemic, and reform without redesign is doomed.
- A post-scarcity economic vision — one that replaces GDP with well-being, markets with mutuality, and competition with care-based provisioning.
- Detailed legislative models, including a full U.S. draft law (*The Post-Scarcity Economic Transformation Act*) and a groundbreaking UN resolution (*The Declaration for the Advancement of Economic and Ecological Abundance for All Peoples*).
- The Trillionaire Stewardship Act — a daring but enforceable proposal: anyone whose wealth exceeds $1 trillion must fund and serve on a global committee to eliminate hunger and water scarcity — or face progressive wealth penalties. Extreme wealth becomes a public duty, not private indulgence.
- A new Universal Declaration of Economic Rights, complete with implementation strategies, sufficiency metrics, and accountability mechanisms — because rights without resources are rhetoric.
- Charters for cities, cooperatives, and communities ready to start now — including

participatory governance templates, regenerative budgeting guides, and commons-based provisioning systems that bypass traditional bureaucracies.
- A roadmap to 2100 — decade-by-decade milestones for moving from emergency response to sufficiency infrastructure to global abundance.

Why This Book Matters Now:

We are standing at the edge of ecological collapse, democratic erosion, and soul-deep exhaustion. Traditional economics has failed. Incrementalism is obsolete. But despair is not strategy.

Reclaiming the Future insists on a different approach: one rooted in moral imagination and institutional design. It reminds us that poverty is not natural, hunger is not inevitable, and the future is not yet written.

This book is for:

- Activists ready to scale their organizing into systems change
- Economists and public servants seeking a bold but viable policy agenda
- Teachers, artists, and thinkers shaping the next cultural narrative
- Community leaders crafting new models of care, cooperation, and commons
- Every person who has ever asked, *"Why do we allow this?"* and *"What can we do instead?"*

From scarcity to sufficiency. From despair to design. From critique to creation.

Reclaiming the Future is not just a book — it's a manifesto, a playbook, a legal toolkit, and an open invitation to participate in the making of a world where everyone has enough, and no one is left behind.

This is the book we've been waiting for.

And now, the waiting is over.

WHY THIS BOOK, WHY NOW

My Journey From the Halls of Power to the Heart of the Problem

I didn't start out trying to overhaul the global economy. In fact, I once thought the peak of civic contribution was getting a legislative bill passed before the end of the next legislative session. But after more than a decade in public service — as a state legislator, policy advisor, and champion of what I fondly (and wearily) call "hopeful legislation" — I realized something was broken far beyond closing some loopholes or filling potholes.

And I don't mean the usual talking points: gridlock, partisanship, or lobbyist overload. I mean *the system itself*. I started asking the kind of questions that lose you friends at fundraising dinners. Why are millions dying of starvation every year when there's more than enough food to feed everyone on the planet? Why is poverty still treated like a personal failure when it's structurally guaranteed? Why does "balanced budgeting" still ignore ecological collapse? Why are we counting GDP while people count the days until their insulin runs out?

This book was born not just from my experience in politics, but from the limits of that experience. I helped pass bills, negotiated across aisles, and celebrated every micro-win like it was the Super Bowl. But deep down, I knew we were rearranging furniture in a house with a crumbling foundation. No matter how cleverly I maneuvered within the system, the system remained allergic to justice at scale.

You might call this book my professional midlife crisis. Instead of buying a sports car, I started diagramming a question that felt both moral and systemic:

"What would it actually take — legally, economically, institutionally — to ensure every human being had access to the basics of life without destroying the planet?"

Spoiler alert: It takes more than a bill or a ballot. It takes a blueprint.

That's what you're holding.

The Moral Imperative of This Moment

We live in a time of contradictions. Hundreds of billions of dollars and very soon a trillion dollars can be hoarded in a private bank account while a child dies from drinking unsanitary water. Our planetary abundance — in food, knowledge, energy, and innovation — is more than enough to meet every human need. And yet billions are still excluded from that abundance by *design*, not accident.

Economists call it "market failure." Sociologists call it "structural inequality." As a dad, I call it what I'd say if my teenager tried to justify hoarding all the cookies while his sibling starved: unacceptable.

This book takes seriously the premise that hunger and water scarcity are not mysteries — they're policy outcomes. We know what causes them. We even know how to end them. The question is: *Do we have the courage and creativity to restructure the rules?*

We're standing on the cusp of a civilizational crossroads. On one path: accelerating inequality, ecological devastation, and governance paralysis. On the other: a world designed not for extraction, but for regeneration. A post-scarcity future where everyone — not just the privileged — has access to the fundamentals of a dignified life.

I don't pretend that this is easy. The transformation proposed in these pages will require legal rewiring, institutional repurposing, and cultural reimagination. It demands new treaties, new metrics, new economic logic. It also demands *you*— whether you're a student, a senator, a CEO, or a civic rebel with a cause.

Because — let's be honest — we're not waiting on billionaires or trillionaires to save us (though I *do* have some notes for them). We're building the new world ourselves, one law, one network, one bold redesign at a time.

From Spectator to Co-Creator — A Personal Invitation

So here's my invitation to you — and yes, I mean *you*, even if you just picked this book up in the airport bookstore because the title sounded like a utopian TED Talk.

This book is not a passive read. It's a participatory one. You're not here to be inspired — though inspiration is welcome. You're here to become a co-architect of the post-scarcity era.

Throughout this book, you'll find:

- Case studies of where transformation is already happening — from Flint to Nairobi, Seoul to São Paulo.
- Model legislation you can use, adapt, or advocate for in your own city or nation.
- A global framework that includes real enforcement mechanisms — including

the *Trillionaire Club*, my cheekily named but dead-serious proposal to ensure those with world-altering wealth take on world-saving responsibility.
- A Reader Toolkit, because change isn't just made in policy chambers — it's made in classrooms, living rooms, city halls, and co-ops.

I've written this not only as a scholar or legislator, but as someone who believes moral imagination is the most underrated tool of our time. If we can imagine better, we can legislate better. If we can name what is unjust, we can dismantle it. And if we build the right structures, we won't have to beg for crumbs — we'll have a feast of justice.

One final note before we dive in: yes, there are jokes. Yes, there are moments where you might throw the book across the room because the truth hurts. That's okay. The old world is cracking. Our job is to write the blueprints for the new one.

So grab your metaphorical hard hat. Let's reclaim the future — not later. *Now.*

What You'll Find in Each Chapter

Each chapter follows a consistent, three-part format to balance storytelling, systems insight, and action strategy. Here's what to expect:

1. Vignette

Every chapter begins with a short human story — real or dramatized — rooted in a lived experience of structural violence, civic transformation, or post-scarcity innovation. These are not just warm-up anecdotes. They are narrative portals into the larger system at stake.

For example:

- A Detroit mother facing water shutoffs.
- A rural nurse overwhelmed by the opioid crisis.
- A Kenyan urban farmer rethinking health from the soil up.
- A youth climate activist in Japan mobilizing global treaties.

These stories humanize the data, frame the themes, and — if I've done my job — stay with you long after the chapter ends.

2. Systems Analysis

After the vignette, each chapter dives into the nuts and bolts, combining:

- Interdisciplinary research from economics, sociology, political science, and public health.
- Historical case studies and policy failures.
- New conceptual tools like "post-scarcity," "commons-based governance," "Universal Basic Services," and "The Trillionaire Club Index."

This is where the sausage gets made — and yes, it's organic, plant-based, and ethically sourced.

3. Applied Solutions

Every chapter closes with grounded proposals — some tested, some visionary:

- Legislative blueprints (e.g., Economic Bill of Rights 2.0).
- Institutional rewiring strategies (e.g., retooling the Federal Reserve).
- Treaties and charters (e.g., GEOA, Post-Scarcity Cities).

- Public tools (e.g., participatory budget platforms, policy co-design software).
- Enforcement mechanisms (e.g., Trillionaire auditing and civic dashboards).

Think of this as the "what to do next" part — because naming injustice without crafting remedy is just eloquent nihilism.

Tools, Humor, and Collaboration — What Makes This Book Different

I've read a lot of books about economic theory and global justice — many of them written by brilliant people who forgot that readers are human beings, not PDF download stations.

This book does it differently — and yes, I take a few risks along the way:

Humor with Purpose:

You'll find dad jokes, dry wit, and the occasional pun about asset bubbles or GDP (Grossly Distorted Priorities). Laughter is a survival skill when confronting planetary-scale absurdities.

Open-Source Models:

We know systems thinking can feel abstract. You're invited to remix and adapt any part of this book's content — because justice is not proprietary.

Take Action:

Change isn't a solo act.

So yes — you can read this book on the couch. But it's designed to follow you into classrooms, council chambers, policy labs, and movement meetings.

Whether you read it in one weekend or one chapter per

month, just remember: this isn't a book about what might happen. It's a book about what's already possible — and the only missing piece is *you*.

1
THE LEGACY OF STRUCTURAL VIOLENCE

Vignette: Maria's Water Shutoff in Detroit

Maria Lopez never imagined that turning on her kitchen faucet would one day yield nothing but a hollow wheeze of dry pipes — or that her child's bath time would require bottled water she'd rationed from the corner store.

A single mother of three living on the east side of Detroit, Maria worked two part-time jobs — neither of which offered health insurance or paid leave. When her youngest daughter caught pneumonia that winter, Maria had no choice but to stay home. She missed a week of wages. That gap was enough to fall behind on her water bill.

Weeks later, a city contractor came. He didn't knock. He didn't ask questions. He simply bent down, opened the valve box by the curb, and turned off the flow. One twist. One decision. One family — cut off.

In Detroit, thousands of residents like Maria have had their water shut off for unpaid bills — sometimes over as little as $150. No due process hearing. No hardship consideration. Just a shutoff notice taped to the door like a threat dressed in bureaucratic language.

Maria's story is not unique. It's disturbingly common — particularly in Black and working-class neighborhoods. The irony, of course, is that Detroit sits on the edge of the Great Lakes, one of the largest freshwater reserves in the world. And yet, for tens of thousands of residents, access to that water is rationed like a luxury item.

Her children didn't understand why they couldn't flush the toilet or wash their hands. Maria didn't have the heart to explain that in one of the richest countries on Earth, clean water had become a *privilege*, not a right.

No court had found her guilty. No crime had been committed. But in the eyes of the system, her inability to pay was a moral failure — one punishable by dehydration, shame, and silence.

Her crime was poverty. Her sentence was thirst.

And the system that handed it down? Entirely legal.

Capitalism's Embedded Inequities and Racialized Exploitation

To understand how structural violence operates, we must begin not with ideology, but with architecture — the design of systems that dictate who thrives, who survives, and who is expendable. Modern capitalism, particularly in its neoliberal and financialized form, is not a neutral engine of productivity. It is a hierarchical operating system. And like all systems, it distributes burdens and benefits along predictable lines.

Let's not romanticize capitalism. It has produced unprecedented levels of wealth, yes — but concentrated in fewer hands than any other system since feudalism. It has scaled innovation, but at the price of ecological collapse. It has increased average life expectancies in some regions while hollowing out entire communities in others. But most fundamentally, capitalism has *never* functioned without a ready supply of human expendability — and historically, that expendability has been racialized.

From the birth of mercantile empires to the present-day gig economy, the engines of capitalist growth have required *somebody else's* land, *somebody else's* labor, and *somebody else's* suffering. This pattern is not an aberration — it is foundational. Capitalism's original sin was colonial extraction: the seizure of Indigenous land, the forced labor of enslaved Africans, and the resource plundering of the Global South to fuel industrial booms in the North.

In the United States, this foundational inequality was codified into law through slave codes, land allotment acts, redlining, and segregated education. Economic apartheid wasn't just social — it was systemic. Generational wealth accumulation was engineered to flow toward white households and away from Black, brown, and Indigenous communities. And when legal segregation ended, economic segregation metastasized through zoning, credit access, labor market stratification, and, as in Maria's case, the commodification of essential services like water.

Capitalism's inequities are most visible in moments of crisis. Take the 2008 financial collapse: the housing market imploded due to predatory lending practices that disproportionately targeted Black and Latino borrowers. When the bubble burst, banks were bailed out. Families — especially families of color — were not. In fact, Black households lost nearly half their collective wealth between 2007 and 2013, erasing generations of progress in just a few years. The same pattern repeated in the COVID-19 pandemic: essential workers — overwhelmingly low-income people of color — were lauded as heroes while dying in disproportionate numbers due to systemic exposure and inadequate healthcare access.

It's important to understand that these outcomes are not bugs in the system. They are *features*. When capitalism is unregulated and growth is prioritized over justice, inequality is not just tolerated — it is incentivized.

Nowhere is this more apparent than in the financial sector, where speculative capital moves freely across borders, seeking profit without regard for human cost. Hedge funds can bet on water futures while children like Maria's bathe with bottled rations. Private equity firms buy up affordable housing, jack up rents, and displace tenants — all in the name of "market efficiency." These are not criminal acts under current law. In fact, they're often tax-incentivized.

What allows this system to persist is the myth of *meritocracy*. The belief that individuals succeed or fail based on effort alone is one of capitalism's most enduring narratives. It depoliticizes suffering and moralizes wealth. If you're rich, you must have earned it. If you're poor, you must have failed. This logic becomes particularly insidious when layered over racial hierarchies. It allows policymakers and pundits to explain away racialized poverty not as the outcome of deliberate policies, but as cultural deficiency, bad parenting, or lack of "grit."

But as countless studies and decades of data show, disparities in income, health, education, and life expectancy follow racial and class lines because the *systems them-*

selves were designed that way. In cities like Detroit, access to clean water or stable housing correlates more strongly with zip code and skin color than with personal behavior. That's not a coincidence — that's structure.

Even philanthropy, often touted as capitalism's moral counterbalance, operates within this logic. Billionaires donate a fraction of their wealth to causes they deem worthy — often while avoiding taxes that could fund universal systems. A philanthropic grant might build a school wing in a Black neighborhood, but the tax loopholes that enabled the donation might simultaneously strip that same community of public funding for teachers, books, or mental health services. Charity becomes a performance of concern that preserves the structural inequality it claims to alleviate.

So what does it mean to say that capitalism embeds inequity and racialized exploitation? It means the system distributes life chances unequally from the outset. It means that access to basic needs is contingent on market logic — and that market logic is anything but colorblind. It means that wealth accumulation at the top often relies on harm at the bottom — harm that is disproportionately borne by those historically excluded from wealth-building opportunities.

This is not to say that every capitalist is a villain, or that markets have no role in human prosperity. But we must confront a hard truth: an economic system that tolerates hunger in the presence of abundance, and homelessness in the presence of vacant luxury housing, is a system that has failed the test of justice.

It is this legacy — this quiet, legal, racialized violence — that we must name and confront. Not with platitudes or performative reforms, but with a structural reimagining of what an economy is *for*. Until we do, people like Maria will continue to face shutoffs, evictions, and premature death — not as accidents, but as budgetary line items in someone else's profit model.

In the sections to come, we'll move from critique to construction. But let this be our starting point: any blueprint for a better world must begin by dismantling the scaffolding that made this one so unequal.

Historical Patterns of Systemic Inequality and Global Extractivism

To fully understand the machinery of structural violence, we must examine its historical blueprints. Systems do not emerge fully formed from academic white papers or election cycles. They are built over time — constructed brick by brick through conquest, law, trade, and ideology. And like all structures, they reflect the priorities of their architects.

Capitalism did not arise in a vacuum. It grew from the soil of colonial expansion, fertilized by forced labor, militarized trade routes, and stolen land. What we call "modern economics" has always relied on extractivism — the removal of value (resources, labor, knowledge) from one place or people for the enrichment of another. Often, this process was justified by appeals to racial superiority, divine destiny, or the invisible hand of the market — all useful myths for the maintenance of inequality.

Let us begin with colonialism. The European powers of the 15th through 19th centuries didn't just explore the world — they extracted it. From the sugar plantations of the Caribbean to the rubber fields of Congo, entire populations were subjugated to serve the economic appetites of imperial capitals. Resources were taken, peoples were enslaved, and cultural systems were annihilated — all to generate profit denominated in currencies that never touched the hands of the exploited.

This was not charity. This was not unfortunate byproduct. This was the model.

In fact, much of what we now think of as "economic development" in Europe and North America was financed by underdevelopment elsewhere. As historian Walter Rodney famously argued, "Europe underdeveloped Africa." The wealth of empires was not created independently; it was transferred from South to North, from colonized to colonizer, through coercion and control.

And when formal empires collapsed in the mid-20th century, the mechanisms of extraction didn't disappear — they evolved. Enter neocolonialism: a system in which formal sovereignty may be granted to former colonies, but economic sovereignty remains captured by foreign creditors, trade dependencies, and multinational corporations.

This transition was institutionalized through the Bretton Woods institutions — particularly the International Monetary Fund (IMF) and the World Bank. Though initially designed to stabilize the post-war economy, they quickly became tools for enforcing structural adjustment programs on the Global South. In return for loans, countries were required to privatize public services, cut social spending, eliminate food subsidies, and open their markets to foreign capital.

This was austerity with a flag of diplomacy.

These policies often devastated local economies. Healthcare systems collapsed. Rural farmers were displaced by subsidized agribusiness imports. Water and electricity became privatized commodities. Entire generations in countries like Ghana, Bolivia, and Indonesia grew up with less access to basic services than their parents —

all in the name of "fiscal discipline" and "market integration."

And while these policies were implemented by national governments, they were crafted in boardrooms far from the people they affected. This dynamic — decisions made by global elites, consequences suffered by the poor — remains central to the story of systemic inequality.

At the same time, multinational corporations became the new colonial governors, operating with more financial power than many nation-states. A handful of companies now control the bulk of global seed patents, data infrastructure, energy markets, and even water rights. In many cases, these firms are not bound by democratic oversight, labor protections, or environmental regulations. They answer only to shareholders — and those shareholders are usually already among the global elite.

Let's make this tangible.

- In the Niger Delta, oil companies have generated billions in profits while leaving behind poisoned rivers, destroyed fisheries, and dislocated villages.
- In Brazil, the Amazon is deforested for soy and cattle exports that benefit a narrow supply chain dominated by international firms.
- In the United States, tech giants extract user data and ad revenue while paying little in taxes and resisting even modest regulation.

Each of these examples reflects a global pattern: the profits are privatized, but the costs are socialized. In other words, a few get rich, while the many deal with the fallout

— environmental degradation, labor displacement, and democratic erosion.

Global inequality today is staggering. According to Oxfam, the richest 1% of the world owns more wealth than the bottom 99% combined. But what is more staggering is how *predictable* that outcome is given the historical foundations. The extraction of wealth from the many for the benefit of the few is not a bug in global capitalism — it is its core feature. And the racial and geographic contours of that inequality mirror the old imperial maps with uncomfortable precision.

Even the climate crisis bears the fingerprints of historical extractivism. The countries most responsible for greenhouse gas emissions are largely in the Global North. The countries most vulnerable to rising seas, droughts, and climate-induced migration are in the Global South. Yet global climate negotiations routinely delay funding for climate adaptation, and fossil fuel subsidies remain orders of magnitude higher than global climate resilience budgets.

This is the legacy we inherit: a planetary economy whose logic rewards harm and penalizes care, whose metrics celebrate extraction but ignore exhaustion. An economy where the Global South subsidizes the Global North through cheap labor, ecological destruction, and structural debt. And one where communities of color, both globally and within wealthy nations, are treated as collateral damage in someone else's accumulation strategy.

To name this structure is not to indulge in guilt or fatalism. It is to be historically honest. Only by understanding how systems of inequality were constructed can we begin to imagine how they might be deconstructed — or replaced.

In the next section, we'll explore the embodied consequences of these systems — how structural inequality manifests not just in bank accounts, but in bodies, ecosystems, and lifespans.

Because what good is an economic theory if it cannot explain why Maria's faucet ran dry?

Impacts on Human Rights, Health, and Environmental Justice

If the previous sections mapped the blueprint of structural violence, this one walks us through its hallways — the lived experience of systemic harm as it manifests in human bodies, communities, and ecosystems. Structural violence is not abstract. It is painfully intimate. It shows up in asthma diagnoses, malnutrition rates, maternal mortality statistics, mental health crises, and in the irreversible collapse of ecological systems.

The concept of human rights is often evoked in the face of obvious state brutality — torture, censorship, wrongful imprisonment. But structural violence erodes human rights more insidiously. When housing is unaffordable, healthcare inaccessible, or clean water cut off, human rights are not violated in a single, dramatic moment. They are dissolved slowly, quietly, bureaucratically.

The United Nations' *Universal Declaration of Human Rights* (1948) states that all people have the right to "an adequate standard of living," including food, clothing, housing, medical care, and social services. Yet these rights remain theoretical for billions of people around the world. And notably, the International Covenant on Economic, Social and Cultural Rights (ICESCR) — which codifies these rights more explicitly — has been ratified by 171 countries but not the United States.

This absence of commitment is not accidental. It reflects a deliberate ideological divide: civil and political rights are considered "negative rights" — things the government cannot take from you — while economic and social rights are viewed as "positive rights," requiring investment, redistribution, and structural guarantees. In neoliberal regimes, the former are celebrated; the latter are ignored or dismissed as unaffordable.

But a right that cannot be claimed, enforced, or lived out is not a right — it's a slogan.

Consider the health impacts of structural violence. In the U.S., life expectancy differs by as much as 20 years depending on your zip code — a geographic proxy for race, income, environmental exposure, and access to care. Black women are three times more likely to die during childbirth than white women, even when controlling for income and education. Native American communities suffer disproportionately from diabetes, suicide, and substance abuse — all symptoms not of cultural pathology, but of systemic neglect and historic trauma.

Globally, the picture is equally grim. Over 800 million people still lack basic access to clean water. Millions die annually from diseases that are preventable with routine care and hygiene. Climate change is exacerbating vector-borne illnesses like malaria and dengue in regions ill-equipped to respond. And the COVID-19 pandemic laid bare just how quickly inequality kills — not just in terms of who contracted the virus, but who could afford to isolate, work remotely, or access vaccines.

Structural violence is also environmental violence. In fact, the two are inseparable. The communities most affected by pollution, deforestation, and toxic waste are rarely the ones who created those conditions. In the U.S., predominantly Black and Latino neighborhoods are far more likely to be located near landfills, chemical plants, and industrial corridors. This phenomenon, known as environmental racism, is well-documented and ongoing.

Globally, the pattern repeats. Oil companies pollute the Niger Delta while extracting billions. Mining operations in the Andes poison water supplies. Palm oil plantations in Southeast Asia destroy Indigenous lands. In each case, the decision-makers are far from the damage, while the people most affected are denied both remedy and recognition.

Climate change, perhaps the greatest systemic threat of our time, is both the product and perpetuator of structural violence. Those who contributed least to the problem — low-emission nations, Indigenous communities, the rural poor — are bearing its brunt through floods, droughts, fires, and crop failure. Meanwhile, wealthier nations continue to subsidize fossil fuel industries, delay decarbonization, and treat climate refugees as security threats rather than victims of policy failure.

This is what we mean when we speak of violence embedded in structure. It doesn't arrive with tanks or tear gas. It arrives with spreadsheets, procurement policies, zoning boards, and international treaties. It arrives in the form of pricing mechanisms that value profit over people, and in legal frameworks that declare water a commodity but not a right.

So what are the consequences of tolerating such a system?

1. Democratic erosion: When people see that their basic needs are not met — or worse, commodified against them — faith in democratic systems deteriorates. They disengage from civic participation or turn to authoritarian alternatives that promise order, however brutal.

2. Intergenerational harm: The effects of structural violence are cumulative. Poor nutrition in early childhood can lead to lifelong health issues. Inadequate schooling narrows economic opportunity. Environmental degradation reduces the habitability of entire regions for future generations.
3. Moral fatigue: When entire societies normalize inequality, a collective numbness sets in. We grow accustomed to avoidable suffering. We tell ourselves that "some people just fall through the cracks," forgetting that the cracks are there by design.

The most dangerous consequence of structural violence is its invisibility — its ability to wear the mask of normalcy. A billion-dollar budget that includes no provision for housing the unhoused is not called violent. A pharmaceutical patent that withholds lifesaving drugs from low-income countries is not called criminal. A billion-dollar hedge fund buying up single-family homes is not called theft.

But the human toll is undeniable.

This book is not a eulogy. It is a reckoning — and a proposal. We do not accept that this is the best we can do. In fact, the very concept of "post-scarcity" exists because we *can* meet everyone's needs. The resources exist. The technology exists. What's missing is a new social contract — one that redefines prosperity, reclaims rights, and restructures the rules.

To move forward, we must understand how deep the roots of injustice run. But we must also imagine what could grow in their place.

In the chapters ahead, we begin the work of construction. From Universal Basic Services to new metrics of well-being, from legislative blueprints to the enforcement mechanisms of *The Trillionaire Club*, we will outline a practical and plausible path forward.

But never forget Maria — and the millions like her. Her faucet did not run dry because we lacked water. It ran dry because our systems lacked justice.

It's time to rebuild.

2

THE INTERDISCIPLINARY LENS

Vignette: Josiah, a Rural Nurse in Opioid-Hit Appalachia

At 6:03 a.m., Josiah Evans started his 12-hour shift by zipping up a body bag.

It wasn't the first time, and it wouldn't be the last. In this corner of rural Appalachia — a place with more churches than stoplights and more overdoses than jobs — death by opioid overdose had become a routine part of the nursing rotation. Josiah, who had trained as a trauma nurse in Lexington and returned home to help his aging parents, now found himself performing CPR in trailer parks, administering naloxone in church parking lots, and comforting children whose parents would never wake up.

This morning's death had been quiet. A woman in her late thirties. Mother of two. She'd been prescribed OxyContin for a workplace injury. When the prescriptions ran dry, the pain remained. A neighbor gave her a pill. Then another. Then came heroin. Then fentanyl. Then the funeral.

Josiah documented the death, filled out the coroner's

report, and stepped outside for a breath of air that didn't smell like antiseptic and resignation.

He was tired. Not just from the shifts or the funerals, but from the sheer impossibility of the situation. How does one nurse address an epidemic built not only from chemistry but from capital?

His clinic was underfunded. The nearest inpatient rehab facility was two hours away — assuming the patient had a car and insurance, which most didn't. The public health officer in the county had been laid off. The high school no longer had a full-time counselor. The coal companies that once employed most of the town had long since pulled out, leaving behind blackened rivers, empty homes, and a Walmart that doubled as the town square.

And yet, each death was treated as a personal failure.

Josiah knew better. He saw the patterns. The economic collapse. The lack of public infrastructure. The mental health crises. The criminalization of addiction. He didn't need another webinar on "resilience" or "compassion fatigue." He needed policy. He needed resources. He needed the system to stop pretending it was confused about why people were dying.

The woman this morning hadn't been failed by her body. She'd been failed by an economy that discarded her, a healthcare system that priced her out, and a political structure that blamed her for both.

Josiah lit a cigarette — his only vice, and one he'd sworn to quit each New Year's since 2015 — and muttered under his breath:

"This ain't a health crisis. This is a systems failure with a body count."

He was right.

Public Health, Sociology, and Economics as a Unified Field of Analysis

The opioid epidemic, like so many crises of modern life, is a hydra-headed monster. You can't solve it with a prescription pad. You can't fix it with a single agency or a siloed intervention. It's a crisis that emerges not just from inside bodies, but from the decay of social systems. And yet, in policy circles, we still treat these issues like they belong to isolated domains. One department handles the economy. Another handles health. A third deals with housing — and so on, until the system fails in committee.

Josiah's morning shift in Appalachia should be taught in graduate seminars. Not as a tragedy, but as a case study in interdisciplinary systems failure.

Let's start with public health. Public health professionals, especially in rural and underserved areas, see firsthand how environment, economy, and inequality intersect. The epidemic that Josiah is confronting isn't just about opioid molecules and pain receptors — it's about the collapse of social infrastructure. When people lose access to decent jobs, housing, education, and healthcare, addiction becomes a symptom of despair — not its root cause.

Yet for decades, U.S. health policy has focused overwhelmingly on *biomedical interventions*. This is the domain of pills, procedures, and prescriptions. It's a system optimized for treating *acute* conditions — but woefully underprepared to manage chronic, structural ones. Public health gets relegated to the margins, underfunded and undervalued, especially in non-urban communities. This isn't just a budgetary decision. It's a political worldview — one that privatizes wellbeing and treats health as a personal responsibility instead of a collective good.

Then there's sociology, which tells us that addiction

rates don't emerge evenly across populations. They correlate strongly with social dislocation, economic precarity, and cultural dispossession. In post-industrial Appalachia, decades of de-unionization, mine closures, and corporate flight gutted the economic base of entire counties. What remained was not just poverty, but *anomie* — a breakdown in the social bonds that give life coherence, dignity, and purpose.

Sociologist Émile Durkheim, writing in the late 19th century, described anomie as a condition in which societal norms collapse under the weight of rapid change. He studied suicide rates, noting how social disintegration — not just individual anguish — drives people to the edge. The opioid epidemic is Durkheim's theory in real time. It is not merely a series of bad choices by isolated individuals. It is the product of a broken collective — a community without resources, safety nets, or reasons to hope.

And what about economics? The dominant economic narratives — focused on growth, employment, inflation, and market equilibrium — rarely pause to ask whether the economy is producing wellbeing. GDP doesn't register overdose deaths. The stock market doesn't flinch when a county loses its only emergency clinic. And when Josiah saves a life with naloxone, there's no line in the national accounts to record the human value of that act.

The economic system we have is obsessed with productivity but blind to suffering. It can measure oil output but not chronic pain. It can calculate the future earnings of a hedge fund manager to the decimal — but not the long-term cost of 50,000 annual opioid deaths, each of which ripples through families, schools, and communities for generations.

Now imagine if we flipped the script.

Imagine if economic health were measured not by quarterly profits, but by public health outcomes. Imagine if health policy were evaluated not by hospital efficiency, but by community flourishing. Imagine if sociological insight informed every economic bill passed by Congress — reminding lawmakers that social disconnection is as dangerous as inflation, and far more deadly.

This is what we mean by interdisciplinary governance — a form of policymaking that treats complex problems as what they actually are: *interconnected*. Poverty is not just about income. It's about geography, race, trauma, education, and mobility. Climate change isn't just about emissions. It's about housing policy, agricultural systems, financial flows, and health equity. And the opioid epidemic isn't just about drugs. It's about *everything* — which is why solving it requires *everyone*.

Let's return to Josiah for a moment. His daily work, though classified under "nursing," includes:

- Emergency medical care
- Mental health triage
- Crisis intervention
- Social work
- Transportation logistics
- Public safety coordination
- Emotional labor for grieving families

And yet, his salary doesn't reflect any of that. Nor does the policy ecosystem around him offer comprehensive support. Why? Because the system was not designed to value multidimensional labor — only compartmentalized tasks.

This segmentation of roles and responsibilities — what

scholars call policy silos — is not just inefficient. It's lethal. When housing authorities don't coordinate with health departments, vulnerable tenants fall through the cracks. When transportation planners don't account for clinic access, medical appointments get missed. When economic development ignores addiction and mental health, entire towns become ghost stories with pharmacies.

The alternative is not a utopia. It's simply better governance. A health department that tracks employment and housing data. An economic agency that includes public health officers in budget planning. A Department of Labor that consults trauma specialists before designing reentry programs for formerly incarcerated workers. A rural broadband initiative that partners with mental health clinics to expand teletherapy access.

These are not radical ideas. They're just logical — if we acknowledge that life does not happen in silos, and neither should policy.

The interdisciplinary lens is not merely an academic posture. It's a matter of life and death. Josiah's patients don't need *another* white paper on "opioid trends by region." They need integrated systems that meet them where they live — not where the funding cycles say they should be.

Next, we'll explore how real-life case studies — from the Flint water crisis to income disparities in rural America — reveal the cost of siloed responses and the transformative power of systemic thinking.

Because if a system is failing across multiple domains, it cannot be fixed from within a single one.

Case Studies – Flint, the Opioid Crisis, and Urban-Rural Inequality

Let's begin with Flint.

If you were trying to design a masterclass in

interdisciplinary policy failure, the Flint water crisis would be your syllabus. What began as a routine fiscal decision — a switch in municipal water sources to save money — rapidly metastasized into a public health catastrophe, a racial justice indictment, an environmental crime, and a case study in bureaucratic negligence.

On April 25, 2014, city officials in Flint, Michigan, began sourcing water from the Flint River instead of Detroit's Lake Huron pipeline. Officials assured the public that the water was safe. It wasn't. The river water was highly corrosive. It stripped lead from aging pipes and delivered neurotoxic sludge straight to the taps of over 100,000 residents — many of them poor, many of them Black, and nearly all of them disempowered by a political structure that ignored their protests for over a year.

What makes Flint a paradigmatic example of structural failure is not just the contamination. It's the failure of multiple disciplines — public health, engineering, environmental science, public finance, and democratic accountability — to operate in concert.

- Public health professionals were ignored or sidelined.
- Environmental regulators failed to mandate anti-corrosion treatment.
- City managers, appointed by state "emergency management" protocols, prioritized short-term cost savings over public safety.
- Public complaints were dismissed as "hysteria," particularly when voiced by Black mothers.

And the response? Fragmented. Siloed. Inadequate.

Had there been an interdisciplinary governance model

in place — one where engineers, epidemiologists, community leaders, and fiscal analysts operated collaboratively rather than competitively — the crisis might have been averted. Instead, the water was poisoned, the people betrayed, and trust in government eviscerated.

Now shift the lens slightly east and south — to Appalachia and the Midwest, where the opioid epidemic unfolded under a different yet eerily similar pattern.

In the 1990s, pharmaceutical companies like Purdue Pharma introduced opioid-based painkillers as miracle cures for chronic pain. They assured doctors that addiction risks were minimal. Medical boards, incentivized by profit-driven health insurance systems, promoted aggressive pain management as a clinical priority. Prescription rates skyrocketed. So did overdose deaths.

The initial blame fell on "pill mills" and irresponsible prescribing practices. But as Part 1 showed through Josiah's story, the deeper crisis was not biochemical — it was structural.

- Economists failed to integrate addiction metrics into labor market analysis.
- Health insurers prioritized reimbursement for pills over holistic care.
- Mental health services were chronically underfunded, especially in rural regions.
- Law enforcement, lacking adequate tools or training, criminalized addiction rather than addressing its root causes.

What was needed was a cross-disciplinary, community-rooted strategy: economic redevelopment, trauma-informed healthcare, harm reduction programs, rural broadband for teletherapy, and universal mental health coverage.

Instead, we got finger-pointing, carceral responses, and litigation that enriched lawyers but did little to rebuild devastated communities.

And now, the epidemic has entered its next phase — fentanyl — deadlier, cheaper, and often delivered through supply chains too fragmented for public health departments to track in real time. The death toll continues to rise, not because we lack knowledge, but because we lack integration.

This leads us to the third example: urban-rural income inequality, and the myth of "two Americas."

It's fashionable in political media to depict urban and rural America as cultural opposites — red vs. blue, cosmopolitan vs. parochial, elite vs. working-class. But this binary ignores the systemic connections between urban and rural economies, and the shared vulnerabilities produced by disinvestment, deindustrialization, and political neglect.

In both contexts, we find:

- Disappearing middle-class jobs replaced by precarious gig work.
- Housing markets distorted by speculation and inadequate zoning.
- Public schools underfunded by tax structures that penalize low-growth regions.
- Healthcare systems fragmented, inaccessible, and unevenly distributed.

What differs is the spatial geography of collapse. In cities, inequality manifests in gentrification, segregation, and displacement. In rural areas, it appears as population loss, infrastructure decay, and service deserts. But the drivers are often the same: market consolidation, automation, extractive finance, and policy designed to maximize growth at the expense of equity.

Here's the punchline: urban and rural decline are not parallel tragedies — they are *interdependent outcomes* of the same flawed economic logic.

For example:

- Rural communities grow the food that feeds cities — yet farmers remain in debt, and small-town groceries vanish.
- Cities drive innovation and finance — yet their economic success depends on undervalued rural labor and externalized environmental costs.
- Both depend on energy, water, and infrastructure networks that are failing under privatization and austerity.

An economist might study income gaps. A sociologist might study social isolation. A public health expert might study chronic illness rates. But only by putting these lenses together can we see the full picture — and design interventions that address root causes rather than isolated symptoms.

This is not merely an intellectual exercise. It's a blueprint for action.

Imagine a national policy initiative — let's call it the Human Systems Integration Act — that mandates:

- Cross-agency collaboration at every level of government.

- Shared data platforms linking health, housing, labor, and education outcomes.
- Funding mechanisms that reward long-term wellbeing, not just short-term savings.
- Community councils empowered to co-design local responses with interdisciplinary teams.

Now imagine applying that to the next Flint, the next opioid wave, or the next regional economic collapse — before it happens.

In other words, what if we acted like systems actually matter?

In the next part, we'll dive into the consequences of failing to do so. We'll examine why single-discipline diagnoses produce chronic policy failure — and how whole-system thinking offers a path toward durable change.

Because as we're about to see, the consequences of ignoring complexity are more than theoretical — they're measurable in lives lost.

Why Isolated Disciplines Can't Diagnose Complex Systemic Failure

If a patient walks into a hospital with chest pain, but is seen only by a dermatologist, we wouldn't be surprised if the diagnosis misses the mark. Yet in public policy — the treatment center for societal pain — we routinely approach complex, multi-systemic conditions with a narrow, single-discipline lens. The result is misdiagnosis, mistreatment, and, too often, moral blame disguised as neutral policy.

Consider any of the crises we've discussed: the poisoned water in Flint, the opioid deaths in Appalachia, the widening income gaps between rural and urban communities. Each involves infrastructure, public health, racial history, labor markets, media narratives, and legal frameworks. And yet each is typically examined in isolation:

- Economists debate wage subsidies without discussing trauma.
- Public health officials analyze mortality statistics without factoring in housing precarity.
- Urban planners focus on zoning without coordinating with social workers or educators.

This siloed approach is not just inefficient — it's actively counterproductive. Because each discipline comes with its own set of assumptions, blind spots, and institutional constraints.

Take economics. Classical and neoclassical models often assume rational actors, efficient markets, and growth as inherently good. These assumptions obscure how systemic inequality, trauma, and power dynamics shape human behavior. Behavioral economics has chipped away at this illusion, but most mainstream economic policy is still designed as if poverty were a personal shortcoming, not a structural outcome.

Public health, on the other hand, has long known that "social determinants of health" — things like income, education, neighborhood conditions, and environmental exposure — are better predictors of life expectancy than genetics or medical care. But despite decades of research, public health remains underfunded, under-authorized, and under-integrated into major policy design.

Meanwhile, sociology offers invaluable insight into how norms, institutions, and identities shape behavior — yet it's rarely brought to the policy table. Political science understands governance structures but often ignores psychological trauma. Urban planning tackles built environments without addressing policing, child care, or mental health.

It's like having the world's best orchestra, but with each musician playing a different song.

The result? Well-meaning but inadequate interventions.

- We get needle exchange programs without decriminalization laws.
- We build affordable housing units without integrated transit or school investment.
- We create economic zones without addressing historical land theft or environmental degradation.
- We fund police departments to "respond" to crises that are, in truth, the downstream effects of decades of upstream policy neglect.

And when those interventions fail, the blame falls not on the system, but on the individual. Josiah's patients are told to "get help" — as if help exists in systems where rehab centers have closed, jobs have vanished, and transportation is unreliable. Flint families are advised to filter their water — as if lead exposure isn't already embedded in their children's bloodstreams. The working poor in rural America are told to "retrain" — as if new skills matter in regions with no employers.

This is what happens when we confuse policy management with systems transformation.

So what does systems thinking offer that traditional disciplines do not?

First, it offers context. It treats symptoms not as isolated problems, but as expressions of deeper structural conditions. A rise in overdose deaths is not merely a "public health issue" — it is a mirror reflecting economic, emotional, and institutional despair.

Second, it prioritizes relationships over components. Systems thinking asks: how do elements interact? What are the feedback loops? Who benefits from the status quo — and who pays the cost? This shift is critical because many of our current crises are not the result of a single bad actor or bad law. They are emergent outcomes of interconnected structures operating exactly as designed.

Third, systems thinking resists linear cause-and-effect logic, recognizing that change in one domain often triggers changes in others. For example, a housing voucher program might only work if paired with public transit access, school integration, and legal support for tenants. Remove any one of those, and the whole effort may collapse — not due to bad design, but due to incomplete design.

Of course, systems thinking is not a silver bullet. It can be messy, nonlinear, and difficult to translate into legislative timelines. It can frustrate funders who want short-term deliverables and policymakers who want clear jurisdictional boundaries. But these are precisely the challenges we must confront if we are serious about building a society that values *solutions over appearances*.

The good news is that systems thinking is not new. Indigenous governance models, community organizing frameworks, feminist economics, and liberation theology have all operated from an integrated worldview for centuries. What is new is the opportunity — and the necessity — to bring these approaches into mainstream governance.

Imagine a legislative committee where a public health expert, a trauma therapist, a transportation planner, a climate scientist, and a local artist co-design policy together.

Imagine a funding agency that evaluates proposals based not just on sectoral impact, but on interdisciplinary ripple effects. Imagine a journalism landscape that tells stories through systems diagrams, not just scandal headlines.

This is not fantasy. It is emerging practice. Cities like Amsterdam are adopting Doughnut Economics to balance human needs with planetary boundaries. Countries like New Zealand are using Wellbeing Budgets that prioritize mental health, climate resilience, and social cohesion. Municipalities in Brazil, Spain, and the U.S. are experimenting with participatory budgeting, integrating residents' lived experience into fiscal policy.

And yet, in most national capitals, we are still playing with 20th-century tools in a 21st-century emergency.

That is why this book is structured not by sector, but by system. The chapters that follow are not just themed — they are interlinked. You will find economic policy nested within climate strategy, public health embedded in labor policy, and legal frameworks grounded in psychological insight. And running through all of it is a commitment to dignity, equity, and co-creation.

Because the problems we face are not singular. They are systemic. And so must be our response.

As we turn the page, we move from critique to construction — from analyzing structural violence to building post-scarcity systems that prioritize human rights, collective wellbeing, and ecological sustainability.

In other words, if we're going to solve crises like Josiah's — if we're going to turn pain into possibility — we need to stop playing solos and start building symphonies.

3
WHY REFORM WITHIN THE CURRENT SYSTEM FAILS

Vignette: Tanesha, a Gig Worker Navigating "Opportunity"

It was 6:45 a.m. when Tanesha Rivera logged into her fifth app of the day — just in time to watch the ride requests disappear like lottery tickets in a fixed game. A single mother in Phoenix, Tanesha worked six platforms: rideshare, food delivery, dog walking, freelance admin, grocery runs, and occasionally babysitting via a neighborhood task board. She had no employer, no benefits, no paid sick leave, no guaranteed wage — and, despite working 12-hour days, no savings.

Still, the onboarding videos had promised flexibility, freedom, even financial growth. "Be your own boss," they'd said. "Work when you want." What they hadn't said was that algorithmic management would determine her every move: where she went, what she earned, and whether her account was "deactivated" for things like declining too many requests or receiving a four-star rating instead of five.

She carried three phones. One for work. One for her child's school alerts. One with a cracked screen she couldn't afford to replace — used exclusively for apps that sent out "hot zone" push notifications about surge pricing in her area. Most days, she ate granola bars between jobs and drank from the same water bottle she'd been refilling for a week. Dinner was a luxury. Rest was theoretical.

And still, she was told she was "free."

On paper, Tanesha was an entrepreneur. Her tax forms listed her as an independent contractor. Politicians praised the gig economy for creating opportunity and removing "job-killing regulations." Tech blogs lauded the innovations that had "disrupted" traditional employment. In reality, she was working more hours for less pay, carrying the overhead costs of her own labor, and competing in a race to the bottom where the only winners were the companies collecting transaction fees from her effort.

When she spoke up about low pay and unpredictable hours, she was told to "hustle harder." When she missed a payment on her car — the very tool she needed to earn income — she was hit with fees that compounded like punishment.

She had no HR department. No union. No sick leave. And when her daughter caught the flu, she had to choose between canceling her scheduled gigs or leaving her child with a neighbor who wasn't licensed to babysit but owed her a favor.

The gig economy had promised autonomy. What it delivered was isolation and precarity, branded as innovation.

Tanesha didn't want charity. She wanted stability. But every time she tried to build it, the ground shifted beneath her — by design. What she needed wasn't another app update or corporate training module on resilience. She needed a system that stopped celebrating exploitation as entrepreneurship.

And she was beginning to realize: reform was never the goal.

Neoliberalism and the Illusion of Individual Responsibility

Tanesha's exhaustion isn't the result of a broken system. It's the product of a system working exactly as designed — a system built on the illusion of choice, the burden of self-optimization, and the gospel of personal responsibility.

This system has a name: neoliberalism.

Neoliberalism is not simply an economic policy or a set of budget priorities. It is an ideology — a framework for how we interpret the world, our place in it, and the rules we believe are "natural" to society. It emerged in the late 20th century, fueled by economists like Milton Friedman and political leaders such as Ronald Reagan and Margaret Thatcher. Its core belief is simple: the market knows best.

Neoliberalism reimagines democracy as a consumer marketplace. In this worldview, the role of government is not to guarantee justice, but to ensure the free flow of capital. Citizens are rebranded as "entrepreneurs of the self," and freedom is measured by the number of apps you can use to monetize your labor. It's not about what rights you have — it's about what you can afford.

The most insidious part? Neoliberalism internalizes responsibility. When the system fails, it doesn't admit design flaws — it blames the user.

Can't afford rent? You should've learned to code.

Crushed by student debt? You should've picked a different major.

Working three jobs with no healthcare? Try budgeting better.

Homeless? Maybe you're just not "resilient" enough.

Under neoliberalism, structural violence is recoded as personal failure.

This ideology has become so normalized that it no longer feels ideological. It shows up in how we talk about "deserving" benefits, in the stigmatization of welfare, in the valorization of the "grindset" and hustle culture. It shows up in self-help books, financial literacy workshops, and TED Talks that suggest that mindset matters more than material conditions.

But here's the paradox: if everyone is personally responsible for everything, then no one is politically accountable for anything.

That's how we end up with policies that subsidize billionaires while criminalizing poverty. That's how the gig economy becomes "flexible," even as workers lose health coverage, labor protections, and basic predictability. That's how we justify defunding public schools while blaming teachers for poor student outcomes. That's how we allow an entire generation to be buried under student debt while telling them that education is the only path to success.

Neoliberal reform doesn't fix these contradictions — it masks them.

Reform, in this context, often means rebranding exploitation as innovation. Want to address healthcare? Offer more private plans with high deductibles. Want to reduce homelessness? Launch a startup that rents sleeping pods. Want to address hunger? Partner with a food delivery app to "gamify" donations.

At best, neoliberal reform smooths out some of the roughest edges of capitalism. At worst, it becomes a public relations strategy for corporations and politicians who want credit for caring without changing the core of their behavior.

Even social justice language gets co-opted. Corporations issue Black Lives Matter statements while funding politicians who suppress voting rights. Oil companies sponsor Earth Day events while accelerating climate collapse. Billionaires speak at inequality summits hosted on yachts.

All of it signals concern. None of it shifts power.

Meanwhile, individuals like Tanesha are left to "bootstrap" their way to stability in a world designed to pull the boots — and the ground — out from under them. She is expected to treat her exhaustion as a scheduling problem, her financial precarity as a budgeting error, and her isolation as a networking opportunity.

But what Tanesha is experiencing isn't burnout. It's betrayal.

She's been sold the story of meritocracy: that if she works hard, she will succeed. What she's been handed instead is an algorithm that tracks her movements, a platform that extracts a commission, and a tax code that classifies her as a business — without offering any of the protections businesses get.

That's not reform. That's exploitation with an interface.

To critique neoliberalism is not to romanticize bureaucracy or government inefficiency. It is to recognize that public systems — when designed well — can ensure collective wellbeing in a way that markets never will. But neoliberalism doesn't just distrust public systems. It defunds them, then blames them for failing.

Schools, hospitals, transit systems, libraries — all gutted by austerity, then mocked for being "inefficient." Meanwhile, private alternatives are allowed to cherry-pick profitable clients while leaving everyone else to navigate patchwork safety nets that unravel more each year.

This is why incremental reform fails. Because it tinkers with the mechanics of a machine built to preserve inequity. It adds ergonomic levers to a conveyor belt that still dumps people at the same cliff.

Tanesha doesn't need a mindfulness app or a gig worker tax credit. She needs structural change: labor classification reform, universal basic services, protections against algorithmic discrimination, and a redefinition of economic success that prioritizes stability over hustle.

Neoliberalism will never deliver that. It is allergic to structural responsibility. It can't solve the crises it creates because it refuses to admit they are political. To do so would be to abandon its foundational myth: that everyone is the author of their own fate — and no one is obligated to care for anyone else.

But care is not a luxury. It is the basis of any functional society.

In the next part, we'll look at how neoliberal reforms — CSR campaigns, charitable foundations, and marginal tax tweaks — offer the illusion of change while leaving the core architecture of injustice untouched.

Because if we want transformation, we need to move past patchwork solutions — and start rewriting the blueprint.

The Limits of Charity, Corporate Social Responsibility, and Marginal Tax Tweaks

If neoliberalism's favorite trick is turning structural violence into personal failure, its favorite cover story is reform through benevolence. Enter: charity, corporate social responsibility, and marginal tax policy.

These are the tools by which unjust systems attempt to

rehabilitate their image — without ever altering their architecture. They are the fig leaves of reform: large enough to suggest care, but small enough to conceal the continued extraction underneath.

Let's start with charity.

Charity is older than capitalism. It has religious roots, civic value, and real emotional resonance. No one disputes that food banks feed people, shelters provide warmth, and community drives save lives. But in a systemically unjust society, charity often becomes the currency of moral outsourcing — a way to manage guilt without confronting power.

Consider the modern philanthropic industrial complex. Billionaires accumulate unprecedented wealth through business models that underpay workers, dodge taxes, and exploit public infrastructure — and then use a fraction of that wealth to fund "solutions" to problems their companies helped cause.

Take tech moguls who donate to education initiatives while promoting gig models that erode job security for working parents. Or fossil fuel executives funding climate research while expanding drilling contracts. Or hedge fund managers backing hunger relief after betting on grain futures.

Even when well-intentioned, modern philanthropy suffers from five systemic flaws:

1. It is voluntary. The wealthiest individuals get to choose when, where, and how they "give back." No obligation. No enforcement. No democratic oversight.
2. It is undemocratic. Decisions about public need are made by private individuals in boardrooms,

not through participatory processes or community consultation.
3. It reinforces inequality. Foundations often exist to perpetuate wealth through tax avoidance, asset growth, and donor-advised funds that operate like shadow banks.
4. It silences dissent. Grantees often censor criticism to remain fundable. Activist movements are reframed as "capacity-building initiatives." Radical ideas are tempered to secure "impact metrics."
5. It obscures causality. A housing nonprofit funded by a real estate developer may help the unhoused — while the developer's gentrification projects create housing precarity elsewhere.

This isn't generosity. It's reputation laundering.

Now, move from charity to corporate social responsibility (CSR) — the business-world cousin of philanthropy. CSR programs are the PowerPoint slides corporations use to convince stakeholders that they're "doing well by doing good." They sponsor beach cleanups while polluting rivers. They tweet about Pride Month while funding anti-LGBTQ legislation. They promote racial equity while lobbying against minimum wage increases.

CSR is a $30 billion-a-year global industry. Yet most CSR efforts are designed to protect shareholder value, not redistribute power. Many are "offset" schemes — compensating for harm after the fact instead of preventing it in the first place. Others are pure PR: vague diversity pledges, sustainability reports full of cherry-picked data, or "community impact" metrics that emphasize volunteer hours but ignore labor practices.

At best, CSR distracts from systemic reform. At worst, it provides corporations with social license to operate destructively.

Which brings us to the final piece of the pseudo-reform trifecta: marginal tax tweaks.

Every few years, in moments of public outrage, governments flirt with modest tax increases on the wealthy. We hear about "closing loopholes," "raising top brackets," or "introducing a small wealth tax." These gestures are greeted with breathless headlines and bipartisan debate — and, more often than not, they fail to pass or are implemented so cautiously they become symbolic.

Why? Because the economic and political system is rigged to tolerate extreme inequality as long as it's dressed in plausible gestures of reform.

Here's the reality:

- A billionaire taxed at 2% may still see their wealth grow faster than the working class can earn it.
- A 1% increase in capital gains tax means nothing to someone with armies of accountants and offshore accounts.
- Temporary surtaxes can be reversed with the next administration — or canceled through aggressive lobbying before the ink is dry.

Meanwhile, the tax code remains riddled with benefits for those who least need them:

- Interest deductions for mortgages on second homes.
- Tax-advantaged stock buybacks.

- Business losses carried forward indefinitely.
- Corporate loopholes allowing companies like Amazon and Netflix to pay $0 in federal taxes in profitable years.

Marginal reform assumes that injustice is a bug, not a feature. It presumes that with just a bit more "sharing," the wealthy will behave like stewards, not hoarders. It imagines a world where capitalism can self-correct — through charity, conscience, or calibration.

But structural inequality doesn't correct itself. It deepens over time unless interrupted.

To put it bluntly: you can't redistribute injustice by donation. You have to dismantle the system that generates it.

This is why solutions like *The Trillionaire Club* — a mandatory, enforceable wealth stewardship mechanism — matter. Because unlike charity or CSR, it doesn't rely on the mood of billionaires or the whims of PR departments. It sets a baseline: if you've accumulated more resources than some nations' GDPs, you owe a proportional, audited, legally binding obligation to human rights enforcement — starting with the eradication of hunger and water insecurity.

It is not punitive. It is just.

Because while marginal taxes nibble at the edges of inequality, systems of structural redistribution — universal services, maximum wealth thresholds, participatory budgeting, and binding international obligations — go to the roots.

Tanesha doesn't need a one-time grant. She needs a system that guarantees housing, healthcare, childcare, and income stability — not when someone feels like giving, but as a matter of right.

And the planet doesn't need another greenwashed marketing campaign. It needs an economic transformation that prioritizes sustainability, accountability, and equity — not just optics.

In the final part of this chapter, we'll look at perhaps the most powerful enemy of real reform: entrenched interests and political inertia — the systems that defend the status quo even as it collapses around us.

Because if charity and CSR are the system's velvet gloves, political capture is its iron fist.

Political Lobbying and the Inertia of Entrenched Interests

If charity is the Band-Aid and CSR is the branding, then political capture is the bulletproof vest — shielding unjust systems from accountability, disruption, or even basic recalibration.

This is where reform goes to die.

Because once you've diagnosed structural inequality, exposed the illusion of personal responsibility, and dismissed symbolic reforms, you run into the final firewall: entrenched power. The kind that doesn't just resist change — it rewires the rules so change is permanently off the table.

Let's start with the most overt form: lobbying.

In the United States alone, corporations and interest groups spent over $4 billion on lobbying in 2023 — that's more than the GDP of some small countries. The top spenders? Big Pharma, Big Tech, Wall Street, oil companies, defense contractors, and the health insurance lobby. These are not passive observers of public debate. They are architects of legislative outcomes.

Lobbyists write bills, fund campaigns, commission "research," and run shadow networks that span from congressional offices to media pundits to think tanks. They don't need to control the whole system. Just a few strategic bottlenecks. A subcommittee chair here. A regulatory agency appointment there. A revolving door between government and industry that ensures institutional memory is preserved — and innovation is smothered in its cradle.

In this environment, even the most popular reforms are suffocated. Consider:

- Universal healthcare: Repeated polling shows majority support across demographics — yet it is treated as politically impossible due to the lobbying power of private insurers and pharmaceutical giants.
- Green energy transition: While climate legislation languishes in committee, fossil fuel companies receive billions in subsidies and employ entire fleets of lawyers to stall regulatory enforcement.
- Labor rights: Despite decades of stagnating wages and declining union power, every attempt at strengthening collective bargaining faces coordinated opposition from employer lobbies and "right to work" advocacy groups.

This isn't gridlock. It's design.

The inertia is further compounded by what political scientists call path dependency — the way existing institutions, norms, and investment patterns make alternative systems seem too risky or unfamiliar. Once a policy regime is in place — especially one that favors private markets and deregulation — it develops a gravitational pull. Budgets, bureaucracies, and careers become anchored in the status quo.

Take public transit. Once a city has invested billions in

highways and car infrastructure, any attempt to build rail or bus systems is labeled inefficient, despite the environmental and social benefits. The same applies to education funding, food systems, and energy grids. We subsidize harm, then declare alternatives unrealistic.

This is how reform efforts get swallowed. Not by debate, but by delay. Not by disagreement, but by design inertia.

And behind all of this is the machinery of campaign finance — the lifeblood of elite political control. In systems where elections are privately financed, the very people who benefit from structural injustice are the ones bankrolling both major parties. They don't need to win every seat. They just need to ensure that no serious threat to their privilege gains traction.

This creates a policy feedback loop:

- Concentrated wealth is used to influence lawmaking.
- Laws further entrench wealth and power at the top.
- The cost of campaigning rises, making candidates more dependent on elite donors.
- Structural reforms — like wealth caps, public finance, or economic rights — are labeled "radical," no matter how popular they are with the public.

You can see this dynamic globally, not just in the United States. In countries from Brazil to India, the UK to South Africa, the gap between public will and policy outcomes is increasingly visible. Voters demand clean water, stable housing, and healthcare. What they get is austerity, deregulation, and the celebration of billionaires as saviors.

That's not a failure of democracy. That's a feature of managed democracy — a system where participation is permitted but power remains sequestered.

So how does this play out when genuine reform is proposed?

Three classic tactics emerge:

1. Deflection – "We need more data." This tactic delays action under the pretense of due diligence.
2. Co-optation – "Let's partner with stakeholders." Suddenly, reform is watered down into a public-private partnership that delivers neither accountability nor equity.
3. Delegitimization – "It's unrealistic." Advocates are framed as naïve, radical, or economically illiterate — even when they're backed by overwhelming empirical evidence.

We saw this play out with the Green New Deal, with wealth tax proposals, with postal banking initiatives, and with universal childcare. Each time, political inertia and elite backlash coalesced — not because the ideas lacked merit, but because they threatened entrenched interests.

Tanesha, back in Phoenix, doesn't have a lobbyist. Neither does Josiah in Appalachia, or Maria in Detroit. But Uber does. Purdue Pharma did. Private equity firms that buy up housing? They do, too — often writing the very laws that protect their profits while externalizing social harm.

This is why the system doesn't just fail to reform. It actively resists it.

So, what's the way forward?

We can't rely on moral persuasion. We must structurally weaken entrenched interests:

- End corporate campaign financing.
- Ban lobbyist-to-legislator pipelines.
- Enact wealth taxation with enforcement teeth.
- Mandate participatory budgeting and citizen assemblies.
- Break up monopoly power.
- And most radically — codify human needs as non-negotiable rights, not commodities up for sale.

This is the path from reform to transformation. It won't happen through charity galas or ESG reports. It will happen through legislation, litigation, public pressure, mass organizing, and structural realignment of economic power.

It will also require new enforcement mechanisms — like *The Trillionaire Club*, a global legal framework that doesn't wait for the wealthy to volunteer their responsibility, but demands it.

Because entrenched interests are not just resistant to change — they're funded, organized, and legally protected against it. If we want a different outcome, we need a different system.

Next, we'll begin building that system — starting with the foundations of a post-scarcity framework that rejects managed deprivation and embraces abundance as a political design principle.

4
PRINCIPLES OF A POST-SCARCITY ECONOMY

Vignette: Leif, a Norwegian AI Developer

Leif Sandvik didn't think much about his next meal. Or whether he could afford to take time off when his son got sick. Or whether a trip to the doctor would bankrupt him. These were not luxuries in his life. They were givens.

A mid-career AI systems architect based in Trondheim, Norway, Leif's days were filled with building decentralized machine-learning tools for local governments, open-source platforms, and academic consortia. He loved what he did — not because it made him rich, but because it made him useful.

His children attended a public school with a curriculum designed around both science and citizenship. His partner, a renewable energy planner, worked part-time and volunteered on a food sovereignty committee. Their groceries were locally sourced through a regional co-op. Their apartment was powered by municipal solar — subsidized, like their transit passes, by taxes on Norway's sovereign wealth fund, built from oil profits and now divested from fossil fuels entirely.

Leif's healthcare was guaranteed. His parents' long-term care was covered. His retirement wasn't a question of *if*, but *when*. He wasn't wealthy by global standards — and didn't need to be.

When he visited the United States for a conference, he was stunned by what passed for normal. Colleagues skipping medical treatment because of cost. Parents working multiple jobs without paid leave. Engineers with six-figure salaries still renting. App developers calculating whether they could afford to have children.

It wasn't that Leif's life was free from problems. But it was free from the constant fear of falling through a hole in the floor.

In a panel discussion about automation, a Silicon Valley executive warned that AI could lead to mass unemployment and social unrest if not regulated carefully. "The future is scary," she said.

Leif politely disagreed.

"The future isn't scary," he replied. "Scarcity is. And most of it is artificial."

That was the difference: Leif came from a society that designed for sufficiency. Not just economic growth — but guaranteed dignity.

He wasn't exceptional. His society was.

And that — perhaps more than any algorithm — is what made his future worth living in.

What Post-Scarcity Means – Abundance Without Ecological Debt

Post-scarcity. The term sounds like science fiction — something you'd find in a utopian Star Trek episode or a white paper from a libertarian crypto-futurist. But what if we took it seriously — not as a fantasy, but as a design principle? What if we treated sufficiency not as a miracle, but as a public policy choice?

Let's begin with a clear definition:

A post-scarcity economy is one in which basic human needs — for food, shelter, healthcare, education, energy, information, and meaningful social participation — can be met consistently, sustainably, and universally without relying on coercion, competition, or resource depletion.

In other words: everyone gets what they need, and the planet survives the process.

It's not about infinite everything. It's about enough for everyone, without extracting so much from the Earth — or from one another — that the system collapses.

This isn't idealism. It's physics, ethics, and systems design.

Let's break it down.

1. *The Myth of Natural Scarcity*

Mainstream economics begins with the assumption of scarcity — the idea that human wants are infinite, resources are limited, and therefore, everything must be priced, rationed, or fought over. This assumption underpins supply and demand curves, market logic, and cost-benefit analyses. But it's also an ideological sleight of hand.

Not all scarcity is natural. Much of it is manufactured.

We produce enough food to feed every human being on Earth — and still, over 800 million people go hungry. We have the technological capacity to provide clean water, energy, and shelter to billions — and yet those resources remain locked behind paywalls, patents, and profit margins. This isn't economics. It's organized deprivation.

Post-scarcity doesn't pretend resources are infinite. It simply starts from a different question: *What would it take to ensure sufficiency for all, within ecological limits?*

That requires not just distributing existing resources more equitably, but also changing the systems that determine how value is created, circulated, and used.

2. *Sufficiency Is Not the Same as Austerity*

Critics of post-scarcity often reduce it to a vision of shared poverty — a world where everyone has just enough gruel to survive, but no one thrives. This misreads the proposal entirely.

Post-scarcity is not austerity. It is abundance by design — a model where the basics are guaranteed so that human creativity, freedom, and community can flourish beyond the grind of survival.

Imagine a city where every person has:

- Guaranteed housing — not luxury real estate, but dignified, energy-efficient, well-maintained homes.
- Free public healthcare — not concierge medicine, but universal access to wellness, prevention, and urgent care.
- Nutritious food — not endless consumer choice, but diets based on agroecological supply chains, cultural traditions, and zero hunger.
- Transit, education, digital access, and cultural life — provided as commons, not commodities.

That's not dystopia. That's civilization — or at least what civilization could be.

Post-scarcity doesn't mean everyone gets a yacht. It means no one drowns while others sail past.

It also invites us to reconsider our cultural definitions of wealth. Is a billionaire who owns six vacation homes and a private jet "richer" than someone who has lifelong health coverage, guaranteed housing, meaningful work, and abundant time with family? Our current metrics — like GDP or net worth — can't answer that. They quantify what can be priced. They ignore what makes life worth living.

3. Ecological Debt: The True Constraint

Of course, we cannot talk about abundance without talking about planetary boundaries. A post-scarcity economy must be ecologically literate. It cannot be built on limitless extraction or the fantasy of decoupling growth from environmental impact through technological optimism alone.

Here's the reality: we are already in ecological overshoot.

We're over-pumping aquifers, deforesting at record speed, warming the atmosphere, and driving mass extinction. Much of this damage is concentrated in the Global South, even as it serves the consumption patterns of the Global North.

Post-scarcity does not mean post-ecology. It requires a paradigm shift: from extraction to regeneration, from linear to circular systems, from competition to cooperation.

This is where Doughnut Economics — developed by Kate Raworth — offers a helpful visual. The inner ring of the doughnut represents social foundations (food, water, housing, etc.). The outer ring represents ecological ceilings (climate, biodiversity, pollution). The goal is to operate within the doughnut — a safe and just space where human needs are met without overshooting Earth's limits.

Post-scarcity lives in that ring.

It uses principles like:

- Distributed energy generation (solar, wind, geothermal).
- Regenerative agriculture that builds soil and sequesters carbon.
- Zero-waste design and the circular economy.
- Open-source manufacturing, 3D printing, and local production networks.
- Shared infrastructure that maximizes utility and reduces duplication.

Technological innovation has a role to play — but not as a silver bullet. It must be subordinated to social purpose, not profit. An AI tool that helps optimize urban food delivery for carbon efficiency? Excellent. An AI tool that lets hedge funds arbitrage clean water markets? Disqualifying.

The test is simple: Does this technology serve sufficiency within planetary limits? If not, it belongs in the discard pile — no matter how shiny it is.

In the next part, we'll explore how automation, AI, and open-source innovation can serve — or sabotage — this vision. We'll separate the hype from the potential, and ask whether technology can liberate humanity from scarcity… or whether it will be used to deepen inequality and entrench control.

Because a post-scarcity economy isn't built in the cloud. It's built on the ground — by policy, infrastructure, and the collective choice to design a world that works for all of us.

The Role of Automation, AI, and Open-Source Innovation

If post-scarcity economics is the house we're trying to build, then automation, artificial intelligence (AI), and open-source innovation are the tools lying on the floor. The question isn't whether the tools work — they do. The question is: who holds them, who benefits from them, and what values shape their use?

Because like any tool, these technologies are neither inherently liberatory nor inherently oppressive. A hammer can build shelter or become a weapon. Automation can emancipate workers or automate their exploitation. AI can optimize for equity or optimize for extraction.

It all depends on the governance architecture around the innovation.

Let's take these one at a time.

1. Automation: Freedom or Displacement?

For decades, automation has been framed as a jobs apocalypse — the robots are coming, and they're taking our paychecks with them. This fear isn't unfounded. From the auto industry to warehouse fulfillment, algorithm-driven machines and robotics have replaced millions of tasks once performed by humans.

But the deeper question is this: why hasn't automation led to more leisure, better wages, or shorter workweeks?

The answer: because under a scarcity-based system, the productivity gains of automation are privatized.

Rather than redistribute time, automation has concentrated power. It allows corporations to reduce labor costs while maintaining — and often increasing — output. Instead of sharing the dividends of efficiency through higher wages or reduced hours, profits are siphoned upward and used to buy back stock or pay out executive bonuses.

Meanwhile, workers are asked to "retrain" for jobs that may not exist, in industries that haven't stabilized, using skills they have to finance through personal debt.

But imagine a different model.

In a post-scarcity economy, automation wouldn't be a threat — it would be a liberator of time. Instead of displacing workers into precarity, automation could:

- Reduce the standard workweek to 20–30 hours.
- Allow for universal caregiving leave, education sabbaticals, or creative pursuits.
- Replace rote, dangerous, or emotionally exhausting labor with safer, more fulfilling alternatives.

This vision depends on structural supports: universal basic services, income guarantees, and democratic control of technological deployment. Without those, automation just accelerates inequality. With them, it becomes a tool of economic liberation.

2. *Artificial Intelligence: Prediction, Extraction, or Collective Intelligence?*

AI is often portrayed as a mystical force — simultaneously savior and supervillain. But beneath the marketing hype, AI is a predictive engine: it learns patterns in data and applies them to generate decisions or outputs. Its value depends on who programs it, what data it ingests, and what goals it optimizes for.

In scarcity systems, those goals tend to be profit and control.

- Facial recognition is deployed disproportionately in Black and brown communities for surveillance — not safety.

- Hiring algorithms reproduce bias because they're trained on discriminatory data.
- Credit-scoring AI tightens access to loans for the poor while giving favorable terms to those who least need them.

Even when used in "neutral" systems like traffic optimization or healthcare triage, AI risks reinforcing existing inequalities if not governed with justice in mind. Bias is not a bug in these systems — it's baked into the training data, which is itself a product of historical injustice.

But again, there is an alternative.

AI can be a tool for equity and planning. It can help:

- Model equitable resource distribution.
- Simulate policy outcomes in real time.
- Identify service gaps in public infrastructure.
- Predict public health needs and deploy interventions proactively.
- Support participatory democracy through real-time feedback loops.

In a post-scarcity society, AI would be governed not by venture capitalists, but by public interest frameworks, ethics boards, and commons-based licensing structures. It would serve planning for sufficiency, not optimization for extraction.

Imagine an AI trained to maximize WELLBYs (well-being-adjusted life-years), not shareholder returns. Imagine predictive tools used to prevent homelessness or reduce loneliness, not just optimize warehouse logistics.

That's not speculative fiction. That's policy choice.

. . .

3. Open-Source Innovation: The Infrastructure of Cooperation

While automation and AI often dominate the headlines, open-source innovation may be the most underrated engine of post-scarcity transformation.

Open-source means that the designs, code, data, or tools are freely accessible, reusable, and modifiable. It is the antidote to proprietary control — the public library to Big Tech's gated communities.

Open-source already powers:

- Wikipedia (knowledge)
- Linux (operating systems)
- OpenStreetMap (mapping)
- Signal (secure communication)
- Countless medical research and educational platforms

In post-scarcity design, open-source is foundational because it does three crucial things:

1. Decentralizes power. Communities can build their own tools, adapt them to local needs, and reduce dependency on corporate monopolies.
2. Accelerates innovation. Knowledge spreads rapidly, without IP walls or redundant silos.
3. Builds trust. Transparency reduces manipulation and strengthens accountability, especially for algorithms that affect public services.

Open-source principles can be extended far beyond software:

- In medicine: open-source drug manufacturing, open-access journals, and collaborative R&D.
- In food systems: seed sharing, agroecological data cooperatives, and distributed supply chain tools.
- In governance: open data dashboards, participatory budgeting platforms, and version-controlled legislation.

Think of it this way: the scarcity system treats knowledge as property. The post-scarcity system treats it as a public good.

And in that vision, the Trillionaire Club — our proposed global mandate for ultra-wealthy accountability — becomes not a punitive framework, but a mechanism for redistributing technical capacity to serve human rights.

LET'S BE CLEAR: none of this happens by default.

Automation without policy leads to exploitation. AI without ethics leads to control. Open-source without infrastructure remains niche. These tools require democratic governance, ethical safeguards, and a commitment to collective benefit over private gain.

Because technology alone won't build a post-scarcity society. But it can give us a fighting chance — if we wield it in service of the whole, not the few.

Let's explore what happens when we stop using prices as the gatekeeper of value — and design systems that distribute resources based on human need, social contribution, and planetary limits.

Because the end of scarcity isn't about having everything

— it's about finally building a world where everyone has enough.

The End of Price-Based Allocation Systems

Price is often treated as a neutral messenger — a clean signal of supply and demand. In classical economics, price is how we "rationally" allocate scarce resources. If something is expensive, it's scarce. If it's cheap, it's abundant. The market, we are told, knows best.

But in a post-scarcity framework, that logic collapses.

Why? Because price is not neutral. It's not a mirror — it's a gate. It doesn't just reflect value — it determines who gets what, and under what conditions. And in a world where need and ability to pay are often inversely related, price-based allocation guarantees that those with the most money, not the most need, win access.

Consider some brutal examples:

- Insulin costs under $10 to manufacture, but retails for hundreds of dollars in the U.S. — because lives are allocated through patents and profit.
- Clean water is free from the sky, yet millions pay exorbitantly or go without — because access is determined by infrastructure investment and billing, not human right.
- Housing is overbuilt in luxury units and underbuilt in affordable ones — because developers respond to speculative returns, not social need.

Price doesn't reflect what's important. It reflects what's profitable.

In scarcity-based economies, this is considered efficient. But in a world of abundance — especially of basic goods — price becomes a form of exclusion. It enforces inequality under the banner of rationality.

Let's dig into the three core reasons why price fails as an equitable allocator in post-scarcity design:

1. Prices Obscure Social and Ecological Value
Take two jobs:

- A hedge fund manager who moves speculative capital between commodities.
- A caregiver who helps disabled children with hygiene, education, and social connection.

Guess who earns more? The market does not reward care. It rewards extraction, leverage, and short-term return. Similarly, nature's regenerative cycles — air, soil, pollination, rainfall — are priceless, yet priced at zero until they collapse.

This is not because the market lacks information. It's because the information it seeks is profit potential, not planetary stability or human dignity.

Post-scarcity systems flip the script. They ask: what are the conditions for collective flourishing, and how do we distribute resources accordingly?

This doesn't mean prices vanish entirely — but they are no longer sovereign. Instead, core needs are decommodified, and market logic is confined to optional goods and services — not existential necessities.

. . .

2. Prices Require Artificial Scarcity to Function

If something is free and abundant, markets can't monetize it — so they restrict it.

Examples:

- Water rights are auctioned to corporations, even in drought zones.
- Seeds are genetically modified and patented to prevent replanting.
- Digital access is gated by subscription models, even when bandwidth is abundant.

This is not market failure. It is market design.

Post-scarcity design requires a shift to rights-based allocation:

- Water is a right, not a billable commodity.
- Healthcare is a universal guarantee, not a deductible calculation.
- Information is a public good, not a monetized dopamine loop.

Under this logic, pricing becomes secondary to provisioning. Resources are shared, not traded. Institutions are designed for sufficiency first, efficiency second.

3. Prices Reinforce Hierarchy and Hoarding

Scarcity benefits elites. When prices rise, those with wealth accumulate more — through speculation, rent-seeking, and exclusive access. This isn't incidental. It's the entire business model of luxury economics: build gated worlds of artificial exclusivity and extract rent from everyone else.

Post-scarcity design breaks that cycle. It introduces:

- Maximum income frameworks — capping extreme hoarding.
- Universal basic services — removing survival from market dependence.
- Public provisioning systems — co-designed by communities, not investors.

Some worry this will kill innovation. But the truth is: innovation doesn't require scarcity. It thrives in conditions where people are free to think, collaborate, rest, and take creative risks — precisely what post-scarcity systems enable.

Imagine if the best minds of a generation weren't building casino algorithms for Wall Street — but solving energy distribution, food logistics, and decentralized manufacturing. Imagine if entrepreneurship meant building commons, not capturing markets.

In this world, value is measured not in prices, but in outcomes:

- Health equity
- Carbon reduction
- Time wealth
- Democratic participation
- Intergenerational stability

These are not soft metrics. They are the true engines of sustainable prosperity.

Toward a Post-Price Infrastructure

We're already seeing glimpses of this transition:

- Universal healthcare systems that remove pricing at the point of use.
- Free public transit in cities experimenting with mobility equity.
- Digital knowledge commons like Wikipedia, OpenStreetMap, and public code libraries.
- Time banks, mutual aid networks, and local food cooperatives that distribute value based on trust and reciprocity rather than price.

But to scale these efforts, we must retool the entire economic infrastructure:

- Shift budgeting from line items to wellbeing indices.
- Redesign tax systems to penalize hoarding and reward regeneration.
- Build digital platforms for cooperative planning and participatory resource mapping.
- Enforce post-capitalist trade rules that prioritize life over GDP.

In the framework of *The Trillionaire Club*, this means members don't just "give" wealth voluntarily — they underwrite the provisioning infrastructure for post-scarcity systems. Their assets become guarantees — not gestures.

Because in a post-scarcity economy, abundance is not a mirage. It is a commitment — to redesign how value is measured, shared, and governed.

With this foundation laid, we now turn from theory to application — from the global vision to national pathways. In the next chapter, we explore how the United States could lead this transformation by drafting a new Economic Bill of Rights, legally encoding the post-scarcity promise into constitutional law.

Because the only thing more radical than imagining sufficiency for all — is making it enforceable.

5

REIMAGINING PUBLIC HEALTH AND WELLBEING

Vignette: Asha, a Kenyan Urban Farmer

Every morning, Asha Njeri stepped into her garden before she checked her phone. Nairobi's traffic, politics, and market chaos could wait. First, she needed to greet the kale.

Her plot wasn't big — just 15 meters of once-vacant municipal land nestled behind a block of concrete flats. It had taken months of community petitioning, unofficial negotiations, and a few wheelbarrows of compost before it bore anything edible. But now, a lush thicket of sukuma wiki, cassava, beans, and sweet potatoes stood where rubble once ruled. The kids called it "Asha's jungle."

Asha was not a doctor. She wasn't a nutritionist or a certified public health worker. But she had become something more radical: a community healer through food.

Each week, she distributed produce to about twenty households — elders on fixed incomes, single mothers, families with children. No money changed hands. The only requirement was to show up — to help tend the soil, share meals, or teach someone else what you'd learned.

It had started with her son's diagnosis. At six years old, he was underweight and chronically ill with asthma. The clinic prescribed medications she couldn't always afford. But a local herbalist — part of an informal health collective in Eastlands — told her to start growing food. Real food. Soil-grown, sun-fed, unprocessed.

Within a year, her son's health improved. So did the neighbors'. Blood pressure dropped. Attendance at the local school increased. Kids stopped skipping breakfast. And most importantly, people started talking — about health not as a transaction, but as a shared condition.

Asha kept a journal of questions her neighbors asked. Why do our clinics always run out of medicine? Why are vegetables at the market sprayed with chemicals? Why do we have to choose between rent and rice?

She didn't always have answers. But the questions told her something important:

Public health wasn't just about hospitals. It was about sovereignty.

The ability to grow food, breathe clean air, walk safely, access care without debt — these were the real markers of health. And they didn't come from reforming the clinic. They came from reclaiming the commons.

Today, Asha's plot is part of a city-wide network of community gardens that feed over 10,000 Nairobians. Some are on school grounds, others in abandoned lots. A few are officially sanctioned. Most are not. But they operate with a shared principle:

Health is not something you receive. It is something we build together.

Universal Basic Services – Shelter, Food, Healthcare, Education, Transport

If income is the fuel of market economies, Universal

Basic Services (UBS) are the engine of post-scarcity societies. UBS flips the script on conventional policy by asking a deceptively simple question:

What happens when the means of survival are guaranteed — not commodified?

UBS isn't just about generosity. It's about logic. Why design an economy that rations essential goods through price, scarcity, or competition, when we can provision them publicly, equitably, and efficiently?

In a UBS framework, the basics of life are decoupled from employment, profit, and ability to pay. This doesn't mean uniformity. It means sufficiency — everyone has what they need to live a dignified life, without fear of destitution.

Let's examine each domain.

1. Shelter: Housing as a Right, Not an Asset

In scarcity economies, housing is treated as an investment vehicle. Properties are bought, sold, flipped, and rented based on their return value — not their human utility. This drives speculation, displacement, gentrification, and homelessness, even in cities overflowing with vacant units.

In a UBS framework, housing is publicly provisioned, cooperatively managed, or non-profit regulated. Models include:

- Community land trusts that prevent speculation by keeping land in common ownership.
- Municipal social housing that is dignified, carbon-neutral, and designed for multigenerational living.

- Zoning reforms that legalize density, mixed-use buildings, and participatory design.

Instead of subsidizing private developers with tax credits to build luxury towers, governments directly invest in housing as public infrastructure — just like roads or sewers. And rent caps, anti-eviction protections, and housing-first policies ensure nobody is unhoused in a surplus society.

2. Food: From Commodity to Commons

The global food system produces enough calories to nourish 10 billion people. Yet hunger, malnutrition, and diet-related illness persist — not from scarcity, but from distribution failure and profit-first design.

Post-scarcity food systems:

- Localize production through agroecology, permaculture, and urban farming (like Asha's Nairobi garden).
- Replace subsidies for industrial agriculture with support for regenerative growers and food co-ops.
- Build public food provisioning systems — community kitchens, school meals, neighborhood food hubs.
- Eliminate food deserts with regional planning, mobile markets, and inclusive procurement policies.

In this model, food is a public health good, not a product. Meals are not a luxury; they are a right of membership in the human family.

3. Healthcare: From Emergency Response to Ecosystem of Care

In the U.S. alone, over 40% of adults avoid medical care due to cost — despite the country spending more on healthcare than any other nation on Earth.

This is not a resource issue. It's an allocation failure.

UBS health systems:

- Guarantee free-at-point-of-use care for all — primary, mental, dental, maternal, and preventive.
- Invest in community-based clinics, peer support networks, and decentralized telehealth platforms.
- Train care workers as public servants, not private contractors.
- Shift incentives from treatment to prevention and wellbeing.

In a post-scarcity health system, wellness is not contingent on premiums, networks, or paperwork. It is built into the fabric of society, with the same inevitability as clean tap water or paved roads.

4. Education: Lifelong, Free, and Liberatory

Education under market logic is often about credentialing, debt, and gatekeeping. In post-scarcity design, it's about freedom — the freedom to understand the world, contribute meaningfully, and think critically.

UBS education systems provide:

- Free, universal early childhood care, K–12, higher education, and adult learning.
- Open-source learning materials, broadband access, and multilingual instruction.
- Curricula that integrate ecological literacy, civic engagement, and social justice.
- Strong investments in teachers, libraries, public arts, and local knowledge preservation.

When learning is liberated from market pressures, students stop asking, "What job will this get me?" and start asking, "What kind of world do I want to build?"

5. Transport: Mobility Without Exploitation

In a market economy, car ownership is often the price of participation — in work, in school, in life. But cars bring debt, pollution, accidents, and time poverty.

UBS transportation:

- Provides zero-fare, frequent public transit — buses, trains, bike shares, and paratransit.
- Reclaims urban space from congestion and privatized parking.
- Connects rural communities with clean energy microtransit and community shuttles.
- Funds infrastructure democratically, with participatory planning and maintenance.

Mobility becomes a right of access, not a function of income. It supports mental health, economic participation, and ecological restoration simultaneously.

. . .

UBS is Not Utopia — It's Infrastructure

Universal Basic Services are not luxury. They're the operating system of a post-scarcity society — what allows everything else to function.

They create:

- Resilience in the face of shocks — economic, climate, or health-related.
- Freedom from precarity — the freedom to change jobs, have children, care for elders, or create art.
- Efficiency — through shared systems that eliminate redundancy, profiteering, and overhead.
- Equity — because public goods shrink inequality at the root, not just treat its symptoms.

And contrary to neoliberal talking points, UBS is not unaffordable. In most high-income countries, UBS would cost less than existing subsidy, tax credit, and patchwork welfare systems — and deliver better results.

The question is not whether we can afford it.

It's whether we can afford not to.

In the next section, we'll explore how to treat public health as infrastructure — not a reactive service, but a proactive design for wellbeing, nutrition, and mental health.

Because health doesn't begin in a hospital. It begins in community, policy, and soil.

Public Health as Infrastructure – Nutrition, Preventive Care, and Mental Wellness

Public health is not a department. It's a design philosophy.

It's not what happens in hospitals — it's what

happens before you ever get there. It is the air we breathe, the food we eat, the time we have, the care we receive, the relationships we maintain, and the systems that make all of those things more or less possible.

In a post-scarcity economy, we stop treating health as an industry and begin treating it as infrastructure — as real and necessary as bridges, roads, and power lines. Because nothing functions when people are sick, malnourished, chronically stressed, or living in fear of medical debt.

Let's walk through the three key dimensions of health infrastructure in a post-scarcity system: nutrition, prevention, and mental wellness.

1. Nutrition: From Calorie Surplus to Nutrient Sovereignty

Malnutrition isn't just about hunger. It's also about food quality, access, and agency. In much of the world, people are both overfed and undernourished — consuming ultra-processed food that's high in salt, sugar, and fat but low in micronutrients, cultural meaning, or sustainability.

Why? Because our global food systems prioritize profit over health. Agribusiness monopolies determine what gets grown, where it goes, and how it's sold. Food deserts and food swamps (where the only options are unhealthy) dominate low-income communities. Healthy eating becomes a lifestyle brand instead of a birthright.

In a post-scarcity model, food is treated as first-line medicine, not market inventory.

That requires:

- Universal access to fresh, nutritious, culturally appropriate food — through public provisioning, subsidies, and community gardens.

- Support for agroecology, urban agriculture, Indigenous food systems, and food co-ops.
- Mandatory regulation of the food industry's labeling, additives, and marketing — particularly to children.
- Public investment in free meals at schools, clinics, community centers, and workplaces.

And importantly: nutrition education shifts from individual advice ("count calories!") to systemic awareness. People learn not just *how* to eat, but why the system feeds us the way it does — and how to change it.

2. Preventive Care: Designing Health Upstream

Preventive care is not just about early screening or vaccines (though those matter). It's about redesigning the conditions that produce illness in the first place. That includes:

- Housing that is warm, safe, mold-free, and free from toxic materials.
- Workplaces that respect ergonomics, emotional safety, and work-life balance.
- Transportation that encourages walking, biking, and low-pollution mobility.
- Climate resilience infrastructure — green spaces, shade, cooling centers, and clean water access.

Imagine an investment portfolio not in pharmaceuticals, but in sidewalks, trees, and playgrounds. These might not yield high financial returns — but they reduce obesity, increase lifespan, and strengthen social ties.

Post-scarcity preventive care also means:

- Universal dental and vision care — no longer siloed from "real" health.
- Accessible reproductive care and gender-affirming services as standard, not exceptions.
- Regular health checkups integrated into life events (e.g., at graduation, new jobs, new housing).

The logic is simple: It's cheaper to build health than to treat illness. And it's far more just.

3. Mental Wellness: Healing the Invisible Infrastructure

Perhaps the most neglected (and stigmatized) aspect of public health is mental wellness — yet it underpins every part of life.

Depression, anxiety, addiction, trauma, loneliness — these are not private failings. They are often the emotional residue of systemic injustice:

- Working multiple jobs with no control over your time.
- Losing a home due to eviction or foreclosure.
- Experiencing discrimination, surveillance, or community violence.
- Living with constant uncertainty around health, income, or belonging.

Mental wellness in a post-scarcity society is not just about therapists and medication (though both are vital). It's about structural safety:

- Enough sleep, enough space, enough support.
- Purposeful labor.
- Time for grief, joy, ritual, and rest.
- Communities where people are seen and valued.

Systemic mental health design includes:

- Universal access to therapy, peer support, and crisis intervention, without stigma or cost barriers.
- Publicly funded mental health first responder programs to replace carceral crisis responses.
- Trauma-informed education in schools and workplaces.
- Cultural recognition of grief, postpartum needs, disability, and neurodiversity as part of the human spectrum — not as pathology.

And above all, time wealth becomes a public health metric. Chronic stress is not just a mood — it's an epidemic. A society that never lets people rest is one that shortens their lives while pretending to raise productivity.

Health as a Social Asset, Not a Private Burden

By redesigning public health as infrastructure, we reject the idea that care is a consumer product or personal obligation. We treat it instead as a co-created, collectively funded system of mutual wellbeing.

This doesn't mean a return to top-down bureaucracies. It means participatory planning, regional variation, and transparency — alongside public financing, professional standards, and guaranteed access.

It means that someone like Asha in Nairobi isn't considered "outside" the system — she is the system. Her food forest is public health. Her shared meals are immunization. Her neighborhood conversations are mental wellness sessions.

When public health is properly understood, everybody becomes a health worker — because health is no longer siloed in hospitals. It lives in soil, in policy, in dignity.

In the next section, we'll explore how to measure that dignity — how to design new metrics for wellbeing that replace GDP and market prices with what actually matters.

Because if we want to build a post-scarcity society, we need better questions — and better yardsticks.

Wellbeing Metrics and Ecosystem Indicators

If we want a different kind of society, we need a different way to measure success.

As the saying goes, "What gets measured gets managed." And for the past century, we've measured our economies by a single number: Gross Domestic Product (GDP) — the total value of goods and services produced in a country.

But here's the problem: GDP doesn't care what you produce, who benefits, or what gets destroyed in the process.

- If a community loses a forest and gains a shopping mall, GDP goes up.
- If an oil spill requires a massive cleanup, GDP goes up.
- If we spend billions on prisons, weapons, and traffic collisions, GDP still goes up.

But if a grandmother cares for her grandchild, a neighbor shares a meal, or a forest sequesters carbon quietly in the background — GDP says nothing. No transaction, no value.

In a post-scarcity framework, this is absurd. Because what we care about isn't "growth" — it's flourishing. And flourishing can't be captured by a number designed to track industrial output in the 1930s.

So, what can we use instead?

Let's explore the three layers of post-scarcity metrics: Wellbeing Indicators, Ecosystem Indicators, and Integrated Indices.

1. Wellbeing Indicators – Measuring Human Thriving

Wellbeing indicators assess quality of life across multiple dimensions — including physical health, mental wellness, safety, equity, education, and social connection.

Some examples:

- WELLBYs (Wellbeing-Adjusted Life Years): Measures self-reported life satisfaction multiplied by years lived. It's used to evaluate policy based on how much happiness or suffering it produces.
- HDI (Human Development Index): Includes life expectancy, education levels, and income.
- HPI (Happy Planet Index): Combines wellbeing with ecological efficiency — how much human happiness is generated per unit of environmental impact.
- OECD Better Life Index: Allows countries to compare progress across housing, income, health, community, and work-life balance.

These tools shift focus from quantity to quality — from profit margins to human potential.

Imagine a public budget hearing where officials argue not over dollars, but over how much joy, health, and equity each line item will produce. That's not soft data. That's democratic accounting.

2. Ecosystem Indicators – Honoring the Planet's Boundaries

A post-scarcity economy must function within planetary limits. That means tracking not just what we extract, but how ecosystems regenerate — or fail to.

Key indicators include:

- Ecological Footprint: Measures how much land, water, and energy we consume relative to what Earth can replenish.
- Carbon Budget: Tracks emissions in relation to climate thresholds.
- Biodiversity Indexes: Monitor species populations and ecosystem health.
- Soil and Water Health Metrics: Assess quality, resilience, and contamination levels.

These are not "environmental extras." They're foundational metrics that determine whether any economy — abundant or not — can survive.

When public investments are scored by their impact on pollinators, clean air, or topsoil retention, we realign incentives with ecological wisdom.

3. Integrated Indices – Tools for Holistic Planning

True post-scarcity measurement blends human and ecological data to guide policy design.

Some promising models:

- Genuine Progress Indicator (GPI): Starts with GDP, then subtracts costs from inequality, crime, pollution, and adds value for unpaid care work and volunteerism.
- Social and Planetary Boundaries Dashboard: Developed by the Stockholm Resilience Centre and Doughnut Economics Lab, it maps whether a society is delivering social outcomes within environmental limits.
- Social Return on Investment (SROI): Evaluates policies and projects based on the total social, environmental, and economic value they generate — often in partnership with local communities.

These tools allow governments to make evidence-based decisions about trade-offs, risks, and long-term outcomes — without reducing humans to consumers and the Earth to inventory.

From Scorekeeping to Storytelling

Metrics aren't just numbers. They're narratives. When GDP rises, we're told the country is succeeding — even if suicide rates are up, forests are down, and workers are sleeping in their cars.

Post-scarcity societies flip the script.

- A high wellbeing score is economic success.

- A reduction in stress, burnout, and loneliness is national progress.
- A healthy river, a thriving coral reef, or a rebounding pollinator population counts — even if it doesn't make someone rich.

These new metrics demand new institutions:

- Wellbeing ministries
- Green accountants
- Civic data cooperatives
- Public dashboards where residents help track, interpret, and co-design progress

And they require rejecting the toxic shorthand that says: "If it can't be measured in dollars, it doesn't matter."

Because the things that matter most — love, safety, freedom, community, balance, beauty — have never been priced correctly. Post-scarcity economics doesn't try to put them on a spreadsheet. It puts them at the center of design.

In the next chapter, we begin the transition from theory to action — exploring what it would take to legally enshrine economic rights at the national level, starting with the United States.

Because once we know what we value, we must write it into law.

6

DESIGNING NEW ECONOMIC METRICS

Vignette: Mateo, a Municipal Planner in Argentina

On his morning walk to the municipal office in Rosario, Mateo Álvarez passed three things he always noted, even if no one else seemed to: the number of pedestrians laughing outside the bakery, the fullness of the public compost bins, and the condition of the jacaranda trees near the riverfront.

They weren't official data points. They didn't show up on any spreadsheet. But to Mateo — a city planner working in the Department of Social Integration — these observations told him more about the city's health than a thousand line items on a fiscal report.

Mateo's department had been experimenting with new budgeting frameworks. Gone were the days when they judged a neighborhood by property values and sales tax revenue. Now they were piloting a wellbeing-weighted infrastructure investment model — allocating resources based not just on need, but on how those resources would improve lived experience.

One project focused on installing public benches, shade

trees, and child-safe crossings in a neglected district with few green spaces and high asthma rates. The old metrics would've dismissed it — "low return on investment," "poor tax base," "non-vital infrastructure."

But the new model told a different story.

After six months:

- Primary school attendance improved.
- Neighborhood crime dropped.
- Emergency room visits related to heat exposure declined.
- And — though no survey had captured it — people began lingering in the public square again, talking, laughing, meeting.

Mateo called this "the arithmetic of dignity."

He was part of a growing movement in Latin America and beyond — from Bogotá to Barcelona, Kerala to Wellington — of municipal leaders refusing to measure progress in narrow terms. They were asking harder questions:

- What kind of life are we building?
- Who gets to rest?
- Who breathes clean air?
- What futures are possible for children?

And they were demanding better answers than GDP.

For Mateo, the turning point came after a particularly tense budget season. A local official, resistant to the new metrics, asked him: "Why should we spend money on things we can't quantify?"

Mateo didn't flinch.

"Because the things that make life worth living," he said, "have never fit in a ledger. But they shape the city more than concrete ever could."

Moving Beyond GDP – History, Critique, and the Politics of Measurement

For nearly a century, one number has ruled the world: Gross Domestic Product.

It determines whether a country is succeeding or failing. It guides investment, media narratives, political campaigns, and international diplomacy. When GDP goes up, economists cheer. When it goes down, alarms blare.

But what exactly is GDP?

It was developed in the 1930s by economist Simon Kuznets to measure national output during the Great Depression. Originally intended as a wartime planning tool and a stopgap measure of productivity, GDP quickly became a catch-all for "economic health." It adds together the value of all final goods and services produced within a nation over a period of time — essentially a giant tally of economic activity.

But here's the catch: GDP makes no distinction between what is beneficial and what is harmful.

- If a forest is clear-cut and sold for lumber, GDP goes up.
- If a city floods and requires billions in reconstruction, GDP goes up.
- If a billionaire buys a fourth yacht, GDP rises.
- If a mother breastfeeds her child, GDP says nothing.
- If neighbors care for one another, cook meals, plant gardens, or grieve together — GDP remains silent.

Kuznets himself warned that "the welfare of a nation can scarcely be inferred from a measure of national income." But his warning was ignored. GDP became dogma. Its simplicity made it seductive. It offered governments a way to track performance and project legitimacy — without asking what that "performance" actually produced for people or the planet.

And so began the great mismeasurement.

1. GDP as a Mirror of Market Bias

GDP treats economic transactions as inherently good, regardless of purpose or outcome. A dollar spent on luxury handbags counts just as much as a dollar spent on clean water infrastructure. In fact, GDP rewards economic churn — even if that churn is generated by illness, incarceration, or war.

It reflects market activity, not human wellbeing.

This distinction matters. A country could be growing rapidly in GDP terms while simultaneously:

- Deepening inequality
- Accelerating ecological collapse
- Suffering a mental health crisis
- Displacing communities
- Extracting wealth from women's unpaid labor

But if enough concrete is poured, enough widgets are sold, and enough apps are downloaded, GDP will tell us everything is fine.

That's not measurement. That's myopia with a calculator.

. . .

2. GDP Ignores Distribution

GDP totals everything — but tells us nothing about who benefits.

If GDP grows by 3% in a year, that could mean:

- A rising tide that lifts all boats
- Or a tsunami that drowns half the country and pushes yachts higher

GDP can rise while:

- Poverty worsens
- Wages stagnate
- Working hours increase
- Wealth concentrates in the top 0.1%

In fact, some of the most unequal countries in the world boast high GDP growth — because GDP is blind to power.

This is not an accident. It reflects a broader ideology: that more is always better, and that the distribution of "more" is a secondary concern. But in reality, distribution is everything. A society with modest income and universal access to housing, health, and education will produce vastly better life outcomes than one with high GDP and extreme inequality.

3. GDP Undermines Ecological and Social Value

GDP doesn't measure the cost of depletion — only the speed of extraction. It doesn't subtract the value of:

- Lost ecosystems
- Extinct species

- Polluted water tables
- Burnout, loneliness, or grief

It doesn't reward resilience, maintenance, or regeneration. In fact, it penalizes them.

- Forests that stand are invisible in GDP.
- Communities that care for elders without paid caregivers are invisible.
- A public health system that prevents illness saves lives — but reduces GDP growth.

In short, GDP treats care, connection, and conservation as economic voids. But these are not gaps. They are the foundations of a livable future.

4. GDP Has Become Political Theater
Because GDP dominates headlines and politics, policymakers often chase "growth" at any cost. Election campaigns are run on GDP numbers. Stimulus packages are judged by how much they "boost" GDP. And international standing — even access to credit or aid — is shaped by GDP performance.

This creates perverse incentives:

- Invest in sectors that create fast economic churn, not long-term wellbeing.
- Prioritize GDP-positive industries (construction, fossil fuels, finance) over care work, sustainability, and ecological repair.
- Underfund public goods because they don't generate direct market transactions.

Meanwhile, entire nations are locked into extractive economies to satisfy global GDP metrics — even as their people suffer and their environments collapse.

THE REAL QUESTION: **What Is an Economy *For*?**

GDP answers that question with a shrug. It assumes that the role of the economy is to grow — forever — without asking what that growth does, whom it serves, or whether it's survivable.

Post-scarcity design begins with a different question:

What kind of economy produces health, sufficiency, sustainability, and joy — not just for the present, but for generations to come?

To answer that, we need better tools. Not just new spreadsheets, but new stories, standards, and values.

That's where we turn next.

In the following sections, we'll examine:

- Wellbeing-centered national budgets
- Social Return on Investment (SROI) frameworks
- And the institutional pathways for embedding these metrics into law, policy, and governance

Because the numbers we count shape the futures we build. And we've been counting the wrong things for too long.

Creating Wellbeing-Centered Budgets and Dashboards

What if your national budget looked more like a community care plan than a corporate ledger? What if the question behind every spending decision wasn't "How much growth will this create?" but "How much suffering will this reduce?" "How much health will this build?" "How much time, freedom, joy, or belonging will this enable?"

This is not a fantasy. It's the foundation of a wellbeing-centered budget — a fiscal tool designed not to maximize GDP, but to optimize what matters most.

In a post-scarcity framework, budgets are no longer abstract technical documents. They become moral documents — visible statements of who and what a society chooses to protect, prioritize, and provide for.

Let's examine how this works — from design to implementation — and how dashboards help make it real.

1. The Shift from Line Items to Life Outcomes

Traditional budgets focus on inputs and costs: How many dollars are spent on education, health, infrastructure, defense. But they rarely track outcomes:

- Did children thrive?
- Did neighborhoods become safer?
- Did emissions drop?
- Did loneliness fall?
- Did working-class households gain time freedom?

A wellbeing budget inverts the process:

- It begins with goals (e.g., reduce child poverty, increase community cohesion).
- Then identifies levers (housing, food, school support, parental leave).
- And finally allocates funding according to the interventions most likely to achieve those goals

— based on evidence, modeling, and participatory input.

The result is not just a different budget. It's a different logic.

It treats governance as public care work, not corporate management.

2. The New Zealand Model: A Working Blueprint

In 2019, New Zealand became the first nation to adopt a Wellbeing Budget as its official fiscal strategy. Led by then-Prime Minister Jacinda Ardern, the approach set five key priorities:

1. Mental health
2. Child wellbeing
3. Māori and Pasifika community equity
4. Green transition
5. Digital and regional innovation

Ministers had to demonstrate how their funding proposals would contribute to these outcomes — not just how they would save money or increase output.

Some results:

- Major investment in mental health services.
- Expanded early childhood programs.
- Integrated climate and infrastructure planning.
- Transparent public dashboards to track progress.

While not perfect, the New Zealand model proved that national budgeting can reflect human and ecological priorities— without collapsing the economy or spooking markets.

Other countries, including Wales, Scotland, and Iceland, have begun similar experiments — coordinated through the Wellbeing Economy Governments (WEGo) partnership.

3. Dashboards: Making Metrics Democratic

Numbers mean nothing if they aren't visible, understandable, and publicly actionable. That's where dashboards come in.

Wellbeing dashboards are:

- Interactive platforms showing progress across social, health, economic, and environmental goals.
- Updated in real time or at regular intervals.
- Designed for public input, citizen science, and participatory policy evaluation.
- Often localized — built by cities, counties, or communities to reflect context.

Examples include:

- Amsterdam's Doughnut Dashboard, which tracks performance on both social foundations and planetary boundaries.
- Santa Monica's Wellbeing Index, which uses community surveys to guide resource allocation and neighborhood design.
- Bhutan's Gross National Happiness Index, built on nine domains, including psychological

wellbeing, cultural resilience, and ecological diversity.

The best dashboards are open-source, multilingual, mobile-accessible, and integrated into both policy processes and public discourse. They allow residents to see themselves in the data — and to see where their governments are falling short.

4. From Data to Deliberation

Wellbeing budgets and dashboards don't just improve accounting. They transform governance.

They:

- Force policymakers to justify spending based on human impact, not ideological dogma.
- Expose inefficiencies masked by traditional economic indicators (e.g., high GDP + high burnout = low return on life).
- Invite residents to become co-designers of public priorities — especially marginalized communities historically excluded from budgeting conversations.
- Link policy cycles to life cycles — making it easier to invest in preventive, long-term care instead of short-term fixes.

Imagine a participatory budgeting process where citizens choose between investing in:

- A new jail
- A community healing center

- A youth mentorship and employment program

Using wellbeing metrics, the jail would likely score negative. The others, positive. The budget process becomes moral math, not just financial math.

Implementation Challenges — **and How to Face Them**
Of course, designing these systems requires:

- Data integrity and interoperability
- Staff training across ministries
- Political courage to change entrenched accounting norms
- Guardrails against greenwashing or metric manipulation

But none of this is harder than the systems we already maintain — bloated with wasteful defense budgets, fossil fuel subsidies, and market distortions that produce harm while claiming efficiency.

In fact, the U.S. Congressional Budget Office (CBO), one of the most influential scorekeepers in the world, still refuses to account for climate, equity, or health externalities when evaluating legislation. This isn't objectivity. It's negligence dressed up in neutrality.

A post-scarcity economy can't afford that kind of blindness.

We need scorekeepers who care about the game — not just the numbers.

In the next section, we explore one of the most powerful tools in the post-scarcity measurement arsenal: Social Return on Investment (SROI). This approach turns every dollar into a story — tracking how public spending creates (or fails to create) wellbeing, equity, and sustainability.

Because if we want better outcomes, we need better feedback loops. And the value of a society should be measured by how well it takes care of what cannot be priced.

Social Return on Investment (SROI) as a Standard for Value

Ask a traditional economist how to evaluate a government program, and you'll get a predictable answer: cost-benefit analysis. If the "benefits," often narrowly defined in monetary terms, outweigh the costs, the project passes muster.

But what happens when the true value of a program is emotional, ecological, cultural, or generational?

- What's the ROI of a suicide prevention hotline?
- Of restoring a wetland?
- Of building public trust in a neighborhood healing circle?
- Of lowering asthma rates through urban greening?

Try putting those into a spreadsheet of net present value and marginal productivity.

Enter SROI — Social Return on Investment. Born out of frustration with narrow cost-benefit thinking, SROI is a framework for understanding and quantifying how value is created across human, social, and ecological domains — not just financial ones.

It's not just an accounting trick. It's a paradigm shift: from measuring profit to measuring purpose.

· · ·

1. What Is SROI?

SROI is a method for evaluating how much social, environmental, and community value a project, program, or investment produces — in relation to the resources it uses.

It asks:

- What changes occurred because of this investment?
- Who experienced those changes?
- How important were those changes to their lives?
- Can we assign an approximate value — even if not priced in a market?

Then it compares those outcomes to the input costs to generate an SROI ratio — e.g., "For every $1 invested, $4.30 in social value was created."

But the point isn't the ratio. The point is the story behind the number:

- What improved?
- For whom?
- How was the improvement defined?
- Was it lasting? Just? Regenerative?

SROI helps surface not just return — but responsibility.

2. How SROI Works

SROI typically follows a seven-step process:

1. Establish Scope and Stakeholders
2. Identify who is affected and involved, directly or indirectly.

3. Map Outcomes
4. Define what changes — intended and unintended, positive and negative.
5. Evidence Outcomes and Assign Value
6. Use a mix of quantitative and qualitative data — surveys, health data, focus groups, lived experience.
7. Establish Impact
8. Filter out what would have happened anyway (deadweight), external influences (attribution), and double-counting.
9. Calculate the SROI
10. Use the data to express a ratio or impact narrative.
11. Narrate the Findings
12. Integrate numbers with stories — for funders, community members, and policymakers.
13. Embed Learning
14. Adjust strategy, share findings transparently, and improve implementation.

Critically, SROI is participatory. The people most affected help define what outcomes matter. That means a job training program isn't just measured by wage increase — but also by confidence, community connection, reduced stress, or dignity restored.

3. Where SROI Is Being Used

SROI has been used across sectors and countries to evaluate:

- Homelessness prevention programs

- Youth mentorship and employment
- Restorative justice circles
- Regenerative agriculture projects
- Public health outreach
- Indigenous cultural preservation efforts

Examples:

- In the UK, a homelessness nonprofit found that each £1 invested in housing-first interventions saved £2.50 in downstream costs (ER visits, policing, court fees) — and produced even greater intangible benefits in mental health and stability.
- In Canada, a community arts program for at-risk youth produced $3.75 in value for every $1 invested — from reduced dropout rates to increased civic participation.
- In Colombia, post-conflict land restoration projects were evaluated for their SROI in carbon sequestration, biodiversity renewal, and social reintegration.

These aren't just warm fuzzies. They're strategic insights into how money, energy, and trust flow through a system.

4. SROI vs. ROI: A Moral Reckoning

Return on Investment (ROI) answers: "Did this project make money?"

SROI answers:

- "Did it make lives better?"
- "Did it strengthen community?"
- "Did it repair what was harmed?"
- "Did it create capacity that lasts?"

In a post-scarcity framework, SROI becomes the standard for evaluating not just social programs — but all forms of investment, including:

- Infrastructure
- Tech development
- Climate adaptation
- Education
- Public safety

Imagine applying SROI to:

- Policing vs. conflict de-escalation programs
- Fossil fuel subsidies vs. ecosystem regeneration
- Corporate tax breaks vs. public housing cooperatives

Suddenly, "efficiency" looks very different.

SROI as a Governance Tool

SROI isn't just for nonprofits or pilot programs. It can be embedded into:

- National budget scoring frameworks
- Municipal procurement guidelines
- International aid and development financing
- Impact investment certification

- Corporate social license evaluation

It invites:

- Multi-dimensional accounting: tracking outcomes that matter.
- Long-term thinking: acknowledging that value compounds, even if it can't be monetized immediately.
- Justice-based metrics: ensuring that the benefits go where they are most needed — and that those most affected are part of the design and evaluation.

In the logic of *The Trillionaire Club*, SROI becomes a compliance tool: demonstrating that extreme wealth redistribution creates measurable returns in nutrition, education, housing, ecological balance, and global dignity.

Because wealth hoarded is risk compounded. But wealth structured for regeneration? That's power in the service of life.

Next, we'll leave metrics behind (for now) and return to institutional design — beginning with how the United States might draft and ratify a new Economic Bill of Rights for the 21st century.

Because if we can measure wellbeing, we should guarantee it.

7

DRAFTING THE ECONOMIC BILL OF RIGHTS 2.0

Vignette: Darnell, a Fast-Food Worker in Atlanta

The fryer had been broken for two days, and Darnell was still expected to clock in at 6:00 a.m. sharp.

The air was thick with burnt grease, and the shift manager was already shouting before he tied his apron. He'd learned to tune it out — just like he'd learned to work through back pain, ignore the unpaid overtime, and smile through customer abuse. It wasn't that he didn't have dreams. It's just that survival didn't leave time for them.

At twenty-nine, Darnell held two jobs, rented a studio with no AC, and sent money to his mother when he could. He had no savings, no health insurance, no paid sick days. If he got injured, he'd have to choose between rest and rent. If the bus was late, he'd lose a shift. If he complained, he'd be replaced.

He was told this was freedom.

On paper, he was an "essential worker." Politicians praised him during the pandemic. Brands thanked him in glossy commercials. But when he asked for a raise? A union? A seat at the table? The door closed.

One night, exhausted, Darnell scrolled through an article on his cracked phone. It was about FDR's 1944 Second Bill of Rights — a proposal for economic guarantees: a right to housing, a job, education, medical care, and security against old age, sickness, and unemployment.

He blinked. Then laughed. Not out of mockery — but disbelief.

"Man tried to pass that 80 years ago, and I'm still begging for a lunch break."

He screenshotted the article and texted it to a friend:

"Imagine if this was real."

And that's the point: it can be. But only if we stop pretending that liberty without livelihood is freedom — and only if we are willing to rewrite the contract at the heart of American democracy.

Modernizing FDR's 1944 Vision for Today's Economy

On January 11, 1944, in the midst of World War II, President Franklin D. Roosevelt delivered what would become one of the most radical — and most quietly buried — speeches in American history.

In his State of the Union address, FDR said the original Bill of Rights, while revolutionary, had become insufficient for the challenges of a modern economy. Political rights — like freedom of speech and worship — were necessary, but not enough. True liberty, he argued, required economic security.

"Necessitous men are not free men," he declared.

Then, without asking permission, he laid out a Second Bill of Rights — a bold vision for postwar America that included:

1. The right to a useful and remunerative job
2. The right to earn enough to provide adequate food, clothing, and recreation
3. The right to a decent home
4. The right to adequate medical care and the opportunity to achieve and enjoy good health
5. The right to adequate protection from the economic fears of old age, sickness, accident, and unemployment
6. The right to a good education

It was a blueprint for post-Depression, post-war human dignity — one that explicitly recognized that freedom without economic sufficiency was a contradiction.

But Roosevelt died the next year. The war ended. The Cold War began. And the Second Bill of Rights never made it into the Constitution.

1. What Roosevelt Got Right

FDR understood that the core challenge of the 20th century was not just industrial production or national defense — it was the dignity of everyday life.

He saw that the market alone could not guarantee housing, health, or stability. He understood that democracy could not survive on empty stomachs and unpaid hospital bills. And he had the political courage to say, in public, that freedom without economic justice was hollow.

At the time, the U.S. was riding a wave of popular support for expanded government — Social Security, the GI Bill, public works. The Second Bill of Rights wasn't a leap — it was a logical next step.

But politics shifted. The business lobby mobilized.

Anti-communist hysteria framed economic rights as un-American. And a once-promising doctrine of shared prosperity gave way to neoliberalism, deregulation, and privatization.

What FDR foresaw — the consequences of unmet economic need in a so-called democracy — is now our daily news cycle.

2. What Needs Updating in the 21st Century

FDR's vision was powerful, but it was still shaped by a mid-century industrial worldview. It assumed:

- Full employment as the cornerstone of dignity
- Growth and consumption as unquestioned goods
- A social compact grounded in male-headed households and racial exclusion

A modern Economic Bill of Rights must go further. It must be:

- Post-scarcity in spirit: rooted not in charity or wages, but in guaranteed provisioning
- Ecologically literate: aligned with planetary boundaries, not blind to environmental limits
- Intersectional: acknowledging how race, gender, disability, immigration status, and colonial legacies shape access
- Participatory: designed not from the top down, but with community input, transparency, and responsiveness
- Digital-age ready: accounting for automation, platform labor, algorithmic bias, and data dignity

And perhaps most importantly, it must become enforceable — not a poetic wish list, but a constitutional amendment, legislative mandate, and institutional blueprint.

3. What Would a 21st-Century Economic Bill of Rights Look Like?

Building on FDR's six rights, a modern framework might include:

1. The Right to Guaranteed Basic Services– Housing, healthcare, education, food, water, energy, and public transit are guaranteed without means-testing.
2. The Right to Income and Time Security– A guaranteed income floor, universal paid leave, and maximum working hours to ensure time for rest, care, and participation.
3. The Right to Meaningful Work and Purposeful Livelihood– Job guarantees in public care, climate resilience, and community-building sectors; plus recognition and reward for unpaid and informal labor.
4. The Right to Health and Bodily Autonomy– Comprehensive physical, mental, reproductive, and gender-affirming healthcare, independent of employment or citizenship status.
5. The Right to Ecological Security– Clean air, water, green space, and protection from climate harm as non-negotiable rights; corporations held legally accountable for ecocide.
6. The Right to Knowledge and Digital Justice– Access to education, digital tools, open

information, data privacy, and participatory civic platforms.
7. The Right to Participation in Economic Governance– Worker representation in firms, public co-ownership models, and participatory budgeting at all levels of government.

This isn't utopian. It's overdue.

And just as the First Bill of Rights defined political democracy, a Second Bill must define economic democracy — the conditions under which freedom becomes real for everyone, not just the privileged few.

In the next part, we'll explore constitutional pathways and feasibility for a 28th Amendment — including state-by-state strategies, historical precedent, and legal routes to making economic rights binding.

Because Darnell shouldn't have to read about rights on his phone in disbelief.

He should live them.

CONSTITUTIONAL PATHWAYS and Feasibility for a 28th Amendment

The United States Constitution is revered, referenced, and laminated on classroom walls — but rarely amended. Since its ratification in 1789, only 27 amendments have made it into law. The last time we did it? 1992 — to clarify when Congress can give itself a raise. (In other words, we move quickly when the stakes are personal.)

So, the idea of adding an Economic Bill of Rights — a sweeping 28th Amendment — might seem, at first glance, ambitious to the point of fantasy.

But so was abolition. So was universal suffrage. So was

the civil rights movement. So was Medicare. So was same-sex marriage.

Constitutions don't change because elites grant permission. They change when reality outpaces legality, and the public refuses to accept unjust norms as inevitable.

We're at that moment now.

Let's break down how it could happen — and why the time may be more ripe than it appears.

1. How Constitutional Amendments Are Passed

Article V of the Constitution offers two routes to amendment:

A. *Congressional Route*

- Requires two-thirds of both the House and Senate to approve the amendment.
- Then, three-fourths of state legislatures (currently 38 out of 50) must ratify it.

B. *Convention Route*

- If two-thirds of states (34) call for a constitutional convention, Congress is required to convene one.
- Any amendments proposed must still be ratified by three-fourths of the states.

To date, all 27 amendments have come via the Congressional route. The convention path remains untested, largely due to fears about a "runaway convention" where anything could be proposed.

But either pathway is viable — if politically daunting.

· · ·

2. Legal Precedents for Expanding Rights

Economic rights are often dismissed as "not constitutional," but that's not quite true. The Constitution has long been used to expand the definition of freedom and protection, particularly when public pressure demands it.

- The 14th Amendment (1868) redefined citizenship and equal protection.
- The New Deal era saw the Supreme Court expand federal power over labor, banking, and commerce.
- The Warren Court (1950s–60s) interpreted due process and equal protection to guarantee public education, privacy, and voting access.

If equal protection can require integrated schools, it can also require equal access to housing, healthcare, and income — especially when lack of access disproportionately harms marginalized groups.

In fact, international law already recognizes economic rights:

- The Universal Declaration of Human Rights (Article 25) affirms the right to a standard of living adequate for health and wellbeing.
- The International Covenant on Economic, Social and Cultural Rights (ICESCR), ratified by 171 countries, includes rights to work, education, and social protection. (The U.S. signed but never ratified it.)

A 28th Amendment would bring U.S. law in line with globally recognized human rights standards — and make those rights enforceable in courts, not just in campaign speeches.

3. A Feasible Framework for Passage
How might we get there?
Step 1: Build a Popular Mandate

- Launch a national campaign, modeled after the Equal Rights Amendment and the Poor People's Campaign.
- Engage unions, churches, civic groups, youth movements, and mutual aid networks.
- Use storytelling — like Darnell's — to make the case that economic rights are not entitlements, but justice.

Step 2: Introduce a Congressional Joint Resolution

- Progressive lawmakers draft and introduce a 28th Amendment proposal.
- Example language:

"The United States shall recognize the right of all persons to secure the means of basic human dignity — including housing, health, education, income, food, and ecological safety — as foundational to the exercise of liberty and justice."

Step 3: State-Level Organizing

- Build state coalitions to ratify, beginning with states that have already passed similar

declarations in their constitutions (e.g., California, Illinois).
- Use ballot initiatives to mobilize support, particularly in states with active labor and civil rights histories.

Step 4: Leverage Crisis Windows

- Historically, amendments pass in times of upheaval (e.g., Civil War, Great Depression, Civil Rights Movement).
- Climate disruption, economic inequality, and public health breakdowns may catalyze a new constitutional reckoning.

Step 5: Legal Pressure and Precedent

- Encourage cities and states to enshrine economic rights in local law — creating jurisdictional precedent.
- File strategic litigation to reinterpret existing constitutional clauses (e.g., "general welfare," "equal protection") in light of unmet economic need.

4. Why Now?

Skeptics will ask: why aim for something so big, so hard, so far?

The answer is simple: because every other reform is blocked without it.

- We can't fix healthcare while treating it as a consumer good.
- We can't address housing crises while calling it a market failure.
- We can't solve inequality if wealth hoarding is considered protected speech.
- We can't stop climate collapse if the Constitution doesn't guarantee the right to a livable planet.

A constitutional amendment is more than policy. It is a moral compass, a long-term safeguard, and a source of enduring legitimacy.

Once passed, it can't be repealed by executive order or undone by the next election. It embeds the principle that dignity is not discretionary — and that a society as wealthy as ours has no excuse for letting people starve, sleep in cars, or die from treatable illness.

In the next section, we'll explore how to align this constitutional vision with federal economic policy — designing legislation that integrates economic rights directly into law, spending, and institutional mandates.

Because constitutional recognition without implementation is a symbol. But constitutional recognition with funding and enforcement? That's transformation.

Aligning Human Rights with Federal Economic Policy
Declaring a right is one thing. Delivering it is another.

History is full of grand proclamations that wither in implementation:

- The 15th Amendment guaranteed Black men the vote — but Jim Crow blocked it for nearly a century.

- The Supreme Court ruled segregation unconstitutional in 1954 — but schools remain racially and economically divided to this day.
- The right to "life, liberty, and the pursuit of happiness" has never included a right to not be hungry, unhoused, or uninsured.

So, when we talk about a 28th Amendment for economic rights, we must talk not just about language — but infrastructure. How do we embed those rights into the operating system of U.S. governance? What laws must change? What agencies must evolve? What metrics, mandates, and money must follow?

This is where the rubber of constitutional aspiration meets the road of fiscal, legal, and administrative design.

1. Budgeting for Rights

In a rights-based economy, the federal budget becomes the mechanism by which rights are made real. That means:

- Every line item is evaluated based on its contribution to fulfilling constitutional guarantees.
- Budgets are not constrained by arbitrary deficit limits — but guided by what's needed to meet universal provision goals.

Examples:

- Housing: Fully fund a National Public Housing Initiative with a guarantee of decent shelter for all.

- Healthcare: Expand Medicare into Medicare for All, making comprehensive care free at the point of use.
- Education: Cancel student debt, fully fund public schools, and provide tuition-free higher education.
- Food: Create a Universal Nutrition Access Program, integrating EBT, community farms, and school meal systems under a rights-based umbrella.

In this model, fiscal debates shift from "how much can we afford?" to "how will this advance dignity, equity, and health?"

It's not austerity. It's moral accounting.

2. Legislative Scaffolding

Rights don't implement themselves. They need legal tools.

A federal framework could include:

- The Economic Justice Act: Mandating national and state action plans to fulfill the 28th Amendment's provisions within 10 years.
- The Department of Economic Rights: A new cabinet-level body tasked with monitoring, coordinating, and enforcing rights implementation across agencies.
- Public Enforcement Mechanisms: Just as Title IX allowed individuals to sue schools for gender-based discrimination, citizens must be able to hold the government accountable for

failing to provide housing, health, and other rights.
- The Trillionaire Stewardship Act: As described earlier, this would institutionalize the responsibility of extreme wealth holders to fund human rights infrastructure globally and domestically — with mandatory contribution thresholds and legal enforcement.

Every civil right in history has depended on structure — the Voting Rights Act, the Fair Housing Act, the Americans with Disabilities Act. Economic rights must be no different.

3. Agency Redesign and Mission Realignment

Most federal agencies were built for a different era — one where markets were treated as sacred and poverty as personal failure. To implement economic rights, we need to repurpose and retool the machinery of the state.

Examples:

- **Department of Housing and Urban Development (HUD)**
- *Old role*: Manage housing subsidies and affordable unit programs.
- *New role*: Guarantee the right to shelter through direct investment, land trusts, zoning reform support, and housing-first implementation.
- **Department of Health and Human Services (HHS)**
- *Old role*: Oversee fragmented healthcare programs like Medicare, Medicaid, and TANF.

- *New role*: Administer universal health access, long-term care, reproductive justice, and mental health provisioning.
- **Department of Labor (DOL)**
- *Old role*: Regulate employment, OSHA compliance, and wage standards.
- *New role*: Ensure job guarantees in climate, care, and education sectors — and track national fulfillment of the right to meaningful work.
- **Department of Education (DOE)**
- *Old role*: Disburse school funding, manage testing, and enforce Title IX.
- *New role*: Fulfill the right to lifelong learning — from pre-K through higher ed, debt-free, culturally inclusive, and digitally accessible.

EACH AGENCY GETS a new North Star: not compliance, not budget targets — but the fulfillment of a human right.

4. Embedding Rights into Rulemaking and Regulatory Design

Rights must also guide rulemaking, which determines how laws are interpreted and enforced.

Example:

Let's say Congress passes a Housing for All Act, affirming a right to shelter. Now HUD must:

- Define "adequate housing" using participatory processes.
- Set enforceable standards for affordability, location, accessibility, and safety.

- Require states and cities to submit Rights Fulfillment Plans.
- Audit and penalize discriminatory zoning and real estate practices that violate the spirit of the right.

The same applies across domains:

- The EPA must define clean air and water as rights, not regulatory thresholds.
- The FCC must treat broadband access as a universal service, not a private commodity.
- The Treasury must monitor wealth concentration as a threat to equal economic citizenship — not just an economic trend.

When rights are constitutional, regulation becomes moral stewardship, not technocratic tinkering.

5. Training a Rights-Based Bureaucracy

None of this works without culture change inside government.

That means:

- Training public employees to see themselves as rights stewards, not just policy managers.
- Hiring from impacted communities and investing in democratic public administration.
- Establishing ombudsman offices and public complaint pathways in every agency — so people can report rights violations without fear or confusion.

- Measuring agency performance not by spending efficiency, but rights fulfillment outcomes.

Imagine a future where a housing inspector, a school administrator, and a USDA analyst all understand their role through the same lens:

"My job is to make the Economic Bill of Rights real — every day, for every person, no exceptions."

That's not utopia. That's constitutional accountability.

In the next chapter, we'll explore transformational legislation — policy packages designed to operationalize the rights framework through bold new acts, local experimentation, and universal design principles.

Because once the Constitution guarantees dignity, the law must deliver it.

8
LEGISLATIVE MODELS FOR TRANSFORMATIONAL POLICY

Vignette: Sarita, a City Councilwoman in Oakland

It wasn't the first time Sarita had stood alone in a city council vote, but it might've been the most satisfying.

The motion on the floor? Whether to pilot a universal basic services framework for District 3 — her district. It wasn't just another benefit program. It was a new contract between residents and their local government. Every household would receive guaranteed access to:

- Free public transit passes
- Weekly boxes of fresh produce sourced from local urban farms
- Access to a neighborhood healing center offering therapy, child care, and conflict mediation
- Rent stabilization and emergency shelter access
- Open hours at community kitchens, co-working spaces, and mutual aid hubs

No means testing. No paperwork labyrinth. No proof-of-worthiness.

Sarita had drafted the ordinance after listening to dozens of constituents who said the same thing in different ways:

"We don't need help — we need the system to stop making us beg."

The mayor's office was skeptical. The budget director winced. Editorials called it "radical" and "fiscally reckless."

But the pilot passed — by a single vote. Her vote.

Over the next year, the data spoke for itself:

- Hospital visits for preventable conditions dropped by 18%
- School attendance rose
- Street-level conflict decreased
- Local business patronage grew
- Requests for emergency shelter declined by half

Residents weren't just surviving. They were exhaling.

Sarita knew this wasn't the end goal — it was a proof of concept. A signal to other cities, states, and eventually Congress that transformational legislation doesn't start in marble halls. It starts on the block, in the garden, on the bus route — in places where dignity had been a stranger for too long.

And once you see it working?

You can't go back to pretending scarcity is necessary.

Proposed Acts – Legislative Pathways to Economic Transformation

Let's be clear: the United States doesn't suffer from a lack of wealth. It suffers from a lack of equitable design. We have more than enough resources, talent, and technology to ensure that no one is hungry, houseless, or uninsured. What we lack is a governance framework bold enough to prioritize human and planetary wellbeing over financial abstraction.

This section proposes four legislative acts — each rooted in the principle that sufficiency is not a privilege, but a guarantee of membership in a functioning democracy.

1. The Resource Equity and Distribution Act (REDA)

Purpose: To systemically address wealth concentration, spatial inequality, and underinvestment in marginalized communities through direct redistribution, democratic allocation, and structural repair.

Key Provisions:

- National Wealth Registry: Creates a publicly auditable registry of assets held by individuals and corporations above a certain threshold ($100 million+), modeled after Nordic wealth transparency practices.
- Resource Equity Fund: Financed through a progressive wealth tax, land value tax, and redirected fossil fuel subsidies. The fund would:
  - Invest in community land trusts, cooperative businesses, and restorative land back initiatives.
  - Provide equity-based reparations to historically dispossessed communities, particularly Black, Indigenous, and environmental justice zones.
  - Support democratic capital grants to

community assemblies for local economic design.

Enforcement:

- Managed by a new Federal Office of Resource Justice, with oversight by a citizen-led Equity Commission.
- Tied to a national index of distributional equity — measuring access to housing, land, credit, public services, and democratic control.

Why it matters: REDA challenges the myth that wealth is meritocratic. It treats hoarded capital as a threat to democracy and repositions distribution as a condition for freedom, not charity.

A DRAFT BILL

To establish the Resource Equity and Distribution Act.

SECTION 1. SHORT TITLE.

This Act may be cited as the "Resource Equity and Distribution Act" or the "REDA."

SECTION 2. PURPOSE.

The purpose of this Act is to address systemic wealth concentration, spatial and racial inequality, and the historic underinvestment in marginalized communities by:

- Creating a transparent registry of concentrated wealth;
- Establishing a federally managed Resource Equity Fund;
- Directing funds to democratic local economic institutions and reparative initiatives;
- Structurally shifting resource governance through federal standards and citizen oversight.

SECTION 3. FINDINGS.
Congress finds the following:

1. The top 0.1% of U.S. households now hold more wealth than the bottom 80%, a concentration that undermines democratic governance and equitable development.
2. Historical dispossession of Black, Indigenous, and frontline communities has produced multigenerational poverty and environmental injustice requiring structural redress.
3. Democratic control over capital and land is essential to racial equity, environmental repair, and community resilience.
4. Transparent wealth reporting is essential for fiscal accountability and public trust in taxation and redistribution.

SECTION 4. DEFINITIONS.

For the purposes of this Act:

- "Qualified Wealth Holder" means any individual or corporate entity with net assets exceeding $100 million USD.
- "Resource Equity Fund" refers to the federal fund established under Section 5 of this Act.
- "Historically Dispossessed Communities" includes communities impacted by redlining, land theft, forced removal, environmental racism, or legally sanctioned economic exclusion.
- "Democratic Capital Grant" means a grant made directly to a local public assembly, cooperative governance entity, or municipal equity board for locally determined investment.

SECTION 5. NATIONAL WEALTH REGISTRY.
(a) Establishment.
There is hereby created a National Wealth Registry, under the Department of the Treasury, which shall:

1. Require annual reporting of all financial and non-financial assets held by Qualified Wealth Holders;
2. Be publicly accessible through anonymized datasets, asset categories, and geographical summaries;
3. Be modeled on international best practices in Norway, Finland, and Iceland.

(b) Penalties for Non-Disclosure.

Failure to report under this section shall result in civil fines of no less than 5% of undeclared assets per annum, and criminal penalties for willful fraud.

SECTION 6. RESOURCE EQUITY FUND.

(a) Establishment and Revenue Sources.

The Resource Equity Fund shall be established in the U.S. Treasury and funded through:

1. A progressive annual wealth tax on net assets exceeding $100 million;
2. A federal land value tax on vacant and high-value land parcels;
3. Annual redirection of at least 80% of federal fossil fuel subsidies.

(b) Fund Disbursement.

The Fund shall be administered by the Federal Office of Resource Justice and allocated as follows:

1. 40% toward capital grants for:
    - Community land trusts;
    - Cooperative enterprises;
    - Nonprofit housing developers;
    - Indigenous land rematriation projects.
2. 30% toward direct reparative payments and equity investment in historically dispossessed communities.
3. 30% as democratic capital grants to local community assemblies, municipal equity boards, and public finance cooperatives.

. . .

SECTION 7. FEDERAL OFFICE OF RESOURCE JUSTICE.

(a) Establishment.

There is hereby created a new agency known as the Federal Office of Resource Justice (FORJ), housed within the Department of Commerce.

(b) Powers and Duties.

FORJ shall:

1. Oversee the National Wealth Registry;
2. Administer the Resource Equity Fund;
3. Develop a National Index of Distributional Equity, including access to land, credit, housing, health, education, and public infrastructure;
4. Issue annual reports to Congress and the public.

(c) Citizen Oversight.

A 15-member Equity Commission, composed of residents from frontline communities, labor unions, cooperatives, and reparations networks, shall hold veto and budget reallocation powers over FORJ decisions.

SECTION 8. ENFORCEMENT AND ACCOUNTABILITY.

- All federal grant recipients under REDA must adhere to transparency and democratic co-governance standards.
- The Equity Commission shall establish and enforce participatory governance benchmarks for all capital grant recipients.

- Any funds misused or diverted shall be subject to full legal recovery and public redress hearings.

SECTION 9. AUTHORIZATION OF APPROPRIATIONS.

There is authorized to be appropriated such sums as may be necessary to carry out the provisions of this Act, beginning with an initial budget of $100 billion USD annually indexed to inflation, plus all proceeds from the designated wealth, land, and subsidy reallocations.

SECTION 10. SEVERABILITY.

If any provision of this Act, or its application to any person or circumstance, is held to be unconstitutional, the remainder of the Act shall not be affected.

2. The Public Innovation and Automation Transition Act (PIATA)

Purpose: To ensure that the economic gains from automation, AI, and technological productivity are publicly shared, ethically governed, and used to reduce human precarity — not intensify it.

Key Provisions:

- National Job Transition Fund: Finances income stabilization, lifelong learning, and paid sabbaticals for workers affected by automation. Fully portable and accessible to gig, informal, and care workers.
- Public AI Infrastructure Mandate:

- Requires all publicly funded or publicly impactful AI systems to be open-source, auditable, and designed with justice impact assessments.
- Establishes the People's Algorithm Review Board (PARB) to oversee fairness, bias prevention, and social impact of high-risk technologies.
• Robot Dividend Model: Corporations that automate labor at scale contribute to a Public Innovation Fund — redistributed through Universal Basic Services (UBS), municipal budgets, and cooperative R&D.

Enforcement:

• Transition funding administered by the Department of Economic Transformation, working with labor unions, universities, and civic tech cooperatives.

Why it matters: PIATA ensures that the "robots are coming" doesn't become a sentence of social abandonment. It reclaims technology for the commons, aligning innovation with emancipation — not exploitation.

A DRAFT BILL

To ensure equitable distribution of productivity gains from automation and artificial intelligence, protect workers through transition support, and establish a public innovation governance framework.

. . .

SECTION 1. SHORT TITLE.

This Act may be cited as the "Public Innovation and Automation Transition Act" or "PIATA."

SECTION 2. PURPOSE.

The purpose of this Act is to:

1. Protect workers from technological displacement by funding income stabilization, lifelong learning, and economic reintegration.
2. Ensure that publicly impactful artificial intelligence (AI) systems are ethically designed, transparently governed, and accountable to democratic standards.
3. Establish a fair contribution model from corporations benefiting from automation to fund universal public goods and cooperative innovation ecosystems.

SECTION 3. DEFINITIONS.

For the purposes of this Act:

- "Automation-Affected Worker" means any worker whose occupation, job functions, or income stability is impacted by AI, robotics, or algorithmic processes.
- "Universal Basic Services (UBS)" refers to publicly guaranteed access to essential services including housing, healthcare, transportation, education, and broadband.

- "High-Risk AI Systems" are defined as those impacting employment, credit, housing, law enforcement, public benefits, or health.
- "People's Algorithm Review Board (PARB)" is the independent oversight body established under Section 5.

SECTION 4. NATIONAL JOB TRANSITION FUND.

(a) Establishment.

There is established in the Department of Economic Transformation a National Job Transition Fund.

(b) Scope and Eligibility.

The Fund shall be accessible to:

- Workers in formal, informal, gig, care, and contract sectors
- Those experiencing partial or full job displacement due to automation
- Applicants for reskilling, income support, or transition innovation grants

(c) Benefits Provided.

The Fund shall provide:

1. Income Stabilization: Monthly cash support up to 80% of lost income, for up to 24 months.
2. Paid Transition Sabbaticals: 3–12 month sabbaticals for retraining, caregiving, or civic engagement.
3. Lifelong Learning Grants: Tuition-free access to

public universities, apprenticeships, and certification programs.
4. Portable Benefits: Worker accounts for retirement, leave, and health, untied to employment status.

SECTION 5. PUBLIC AI INFRASTRUCTURE MANDATE.

(a) Open-Source Mandate.

All AI systems developed with public funds or having broad societal impact must be:

- Open-source
- Auditable
- Subject to regular justice impact assessments

(b) Justice Impact Assessments Must Include:

- Historical bias testing
- Equity forecasting
- Labor impact modeling
- Consent mechanisms
- Language accessibility

(c) Establishment of PARB.

The People's Algorithm Review Board (PARB) shall:

- Consist of ethicists, engineers, labor representatives, community advocates, and legal scholars
- Have binding oversight over deployment of high-risk systems

- Be empowered to delay, revise, or suspend use of systems violating public interest standards

SECTION 6. ROBOT DIVIDEND MODEL.

(a) Definition.

A Robot Dividend is a mandatory contribution made by corporations that automate labor at scale, defined as reducing more than 15% of total workforce via automation in any 3-year period.

(b) Contribution Rate.

Corporations shall contribute a rate of 1–5% of net productivity gains to the Public Innovation Fund established under this section.

(c) Use of Funds.

Funds shall be used for:

1. Expanding Universal Basic Services
2. Municipal and tribal infrastructure budgets
3. Open-source, public-interest R&D hubs
4. Worker-owned automation cooperatives
5. Accessibility technologies for disabled populations

SECTION 7. ADMINISTRATION AND ENFORCEMENT.

(a) Lead Agency.

The Department of Economic Transformation (DET) shall:

- Administer the Job Transition Fund

- Publish annual reports on automation trends and intervention outcomes
- Partner with labor unions, public universities, and civic tech cooperatives for local program delivery

(b) Civil Penalties.
Failure to comply with Robot Dividend obligations or AI transparency mandates shall result in:

- Civil fines up to $25 million or 3% of gross automation-related profits
- Injunctive relief by the Federal Trade Commission or PARB

SECTION 8. PUBLIC TRANSPARENCY AND DATA ACCESS.

- A National Open Algorithms Archive shall host source code, audit reports, and usage logs for all qualifying AI systems.
- All transition-related program data must be disaggregated by race, income, geography, age, and disability status to ensure equity.

SECTION 9. AUTHORIZATION OF APPROPRIATIONS.

There is authorized to be appropriated $125 billion over 10 years to implement the provisions of this Act, including:

- $75B for Job Transition Fund
- $30B for Universal Basic Services integration
- $20B for civic tech, algorithmic oversight, and public AI infrastructure

SECTION 10. SEVERABILITY.

If any provision of this Act is found unconstitutional or otherwise unenforceable, the remainder shall remain in full force and effect.

3. The Universal Basic Services Framework Act (UBSFA)

Purpose: To guarantee public provisioning of life's essentials — food, housing, health, education, care, energy, and transit — at national scale, using a constitutional rights-based framework.

Key Provisions:

- Establishes a Universal Basic Services Guarantee, which entitles every resident to:
    - Public housing or rental assistance
    - Free healthcare at the point of use
    - Tuition-free public education through college
    - Publicly supported childcare, elder care, and disability services
    - Free regional public transit and internet access
    - Monthly food credits redeemable at grocery stores, farmers' markets, and co-ops
- Creates Public Commons Infrastructure Zones — municipalities or regions that pilot

full UBS provisioning with bundled funding, citizen planning boards, and community oversight.
- Consolidates and replaces fragmented means-tested programs (e.g., SNAP, TANF, housing vouchers) with universal access, high-trust delivery, and dramatically reduced bureaucratic overhead.

Funding Mechanisms:

- Redirects existing subsidies and tax expenditures that disproportionately benefit the wealthy (e.g., mortgage interest deductions, fossil fuel credits).
- Applies proportional participation contributions from members of The Trillionaire Club when relevant UBS benchmarks remain unmet.

Why it matters: UBSFA replaces paternalistic welfare logic with economic citizenship — shifting the social contract from survival eligibility to universal entitlement.

A DRAFT BILL

To establish a national Universal Basic Services (UBS) guarantee for all U.S. residents, ensuring constitutional access to life-sustaining public goods including housing, food, healthcare, education, care, transit, energy, and digital connectivity.

SECTION 1. SHORT TITLE.

This Act may be cited as the "Universal Basic Services Framework Act" or the "UBSFA."

SECTION 2. PURPOSE AND INTENT.

It is the intent of Congress that:

- Access to life's essentials is a constitutional right, not a conditional benefit.
- Universal Basic Services shall serve as the foundation for economic security, human dignity, and democratic participation.
- Fragmented and means-tested safety nets shall be consolidated into a high-trust, universal provisioning model that reduces administrative waste and restores civic equity.

SECTION 3. FINDINGS.

Congress finds:

1. The United States ranks behind peer nations in guaranteeing universal access to housing, healthcare, transit, and care services.
2. Economic hardship, food insecurity, housing instability, and access inequities are not individual failings but policy choices.
3. A rights-based framework for basic services reduces systemic inequality, improves health outcomes, boosts civic trust, and enhances national resilience.

4. Universal service delivery, when funded and designed democratically, reduces stigma, bureaucratic friction, and long-term public costs.

SECTION 4. DEFINITIONS.

- "Universal Basic Services (UBS)" means publicly funded and guaranteed access to foundational human needs including housing, health, education, food, care, energy, transit, and digital connectivity.
- "Resident" means any individual lawfully residing in the United States, regardless of citizenship status.
- "Public Commons Infrastructure Zone" means a municipality, region, or tribal territory piloting comprehensive UBS provisioning under this Act.
- "Trillionaire Club Contribution" refers to conditional fiscal participation by ultra-wealth holders under the Resource Equity and Distribution Act or successor provisions.

SECTION 5. UNIVERSAL BASIC SERVICES GUARANTEE.
All U.S. residents shall be entitled to:

1. Housing – Access to public housing, cooperative housing, or capped rental assistance sufficient to meet local living standards.

2. Healthcare – Comprehensive, publicly funded healthcare at the point of use, with no out-of-pocket costs.
3. Education – Tuition-free education from pre-K through public university or trade school, including materials and support services.
4. Care – Guaranteed access to:
   - Publicly funded childcare for all parents and guardians
   - Dignified elder care services
   - Fully inclusive disability services
5. Transit and Digital Access – Free access to:
   - Regional public transportation systems
   - Broadband internet as a utility-level public good
6. Food – Monthly food credits redeemable at:
   - Grocery retailers
   - Farmers' markets
   - Food cooperatives

SECTION 6. PUBLIC COMMONS INFRASTRUCTURE ZONES (PCIZs).

(a) Establishment.

The Department of Health and Human Services, in coordination with the Departments of Transportation, Housing and Urban Development, and Commerce, shall authorize and fund PCIZs.

(b) Pilot Program Design.

Each zone shall include:

- Bundled UBS funding with minimum per capita guarantees
- Participatory budgeting processes
- Citizen-led planning boards with binding input
- Data transparency and equity dashboards
- Annual impact reporting to Congress and local assemblies

(c) Selection Criteria.
Priority shall be given to:

- High-poverty urban and rural areas
- Tribal nations and environmental justice communities
- Regions undergoing economic transition or displacement

SECTION 7. CONSOLIDATION OF SAFETY NET PROGRAMS.

(a) Program Consolidation.

The following programs shall be sunset or integrated into UBSFA implementation over a five-year period:

- Supplemental Nutrition Assistance Program (SNAP)
- Temporary Assistance for Needy Families (TANF)
- Section 8 Housing Choice Vouchers
- Home Energy Assistance (LIHEAP)
- Medicaid means-testing waivers

(b) Transition Principles.

- No current beneficiary shall experience a service disruption.
- A unified benefits interface shall replace fragmented eligibility portals.
- Delivery systems must meet plain-language, multilingual, and disability access standards.

SECTION 8. FUNDING AND REVENUE SOURCES.
Funding for UBSFA shall be derived from:

1. Reallocation of federal tax expenditures disproportionately benefiting the top quintile of income earners, including but not limited to:
    - Mortgage interest deduction reform
    - Capital gains exclusion cap adjustments
    - Fossil fuel tax subsidies
2. Progressive wealth taxation as enabled by the Resource Equity and Distribution Act (REDA)
3. Proportional contribution requirements from The Trillionaire Club under REDA Article 9 when national UBS benchmarks fall below minimum thresholds

SECTION 9. ADMINISTRATION AND OVERSIGHT.
A new Office of Basic Services Equity (OBSE) shall be

created under the Department of Health and Human Services to:

- Monitor UBS compliance at federal, state, and municipal levels
- Coordinate interagency funding, delivery, and metrics
- Ensure civil rights compliance in UBS access
- Submit annual public performance and equity audits to Congress

SECTION 10. AUTHORIZATION OF APPROPRIATIONS.
There is authorized to be appropriated:

- $350 billion annually over 10 years to establish and maintain UBS guarantees
- Additional discretionary spending indexed to inflation, housing need, and energy transition benchmarks

SECTION 11. SEVERABILITY.
If any provision of this Act or its application to any person or circumstance is held unconstitutional, the remainder of the Act shall not be affected.

4. Trillionaire Stewardship Act

Purpose: The Trillionaire Stewardship Act (TSA) is a binding global framework that automatically assigns public duties to individuals whose net worth exceeds $1 trillion USD (adjusted annually for inflation and purchasing power parity).

This act treats extreme wealth not as an economic outlier, but as a jurisdiction — a governance condition that triggers automatic obligations to humanity, the planet, and future generations.

Key Provisions of the Act

1. Automatic Enrollment in the Global Committee for Food and Water Security (GCFWS)

- Upon reaching the $1T threshold, individuals are automatically inducted into the GCFWS.
- Participation is not voluntary. It is a legal condition of retaining private ownership of such wealth.
- The Committee is housed under the UN High-Level Panel on Global Development Equity, co-chaired by the UN, African Union, and rotating citizen assemblies.

2. Mandated Contributions Based on a Responsibility Ratio (RR)

- Every trillionaire must annually contribute a minimum of 5% of their net worth (or the value equivalent in liquid capital) toward:
  - Eradication of hunger
  - Provisioning of clean water infrastructure
  - Climate-resilient agricultural innovation
- The RR increases by 1% annually for every year goals remain unmet, up to 15%.

3. Impact-Weighted Obligations

- Contributions are evaluated not just in dollar amount, but social return on investment (SROI).
- If targeted countries or regions do not show measurable reductions in food insecurity and water access inequality, additional assessments are triggered.

4. Governance by Affected Populations

- Spending priorities are determined by Community Sovereignty Forums (CSFs) — assemblies composed of residents from the most affected regions.
- Trillionaires do not control implementation. Their role is financing, compliance, and transparency.

5. Transparency and Global Reporting

- The Global Economic Rights Observatory (GERO) publishes annual audits of compliance, impact metrics, and contribution reports.
- Refusal to comply triggers international enforcement mechanisms including:
    - Automatic global asset tax surcharges
    - Freezing of international investment privileges
    - Suspension of multinational licensing and IP protections

Why Is This Necessary?

The world has crossed the moral event horizon where eight billion people rely on a system in which one person can amass more wealth than 80 sovereign nations.

This isn't just inequality. It's an ecological, spiritual, and democratic crisis.

Trillionaire wealth is not earned in isolation:

- It depends on public infrastructure (roads, patents, schools, the internet).
- It exploits tax havens, loopholes, and debt-based extraction.
- It often exacerbates climate breakdown, monopoly, and political capture.

The Stewardship Act answers this not with charity, but with obligation:

If your wealth exceeds the combined GDP of West Africa, you don't get to opt out of feeding the hungry.

DRAFT BILL
Trillionaire Stewardship Act

SECTION 1. SHORT TITLE

This Act may be cited as the "Trillionaire Stewardship Act of 2026."

SECTION 2. FINDINGS AND PURPOSE

(a) Congressional Findings:

1. In the 21st century, private individuals may possess wealth exceeding the GDP of entire nations, necessitating new models of civic responsibility.
2. Extreme wealth creates structural influence and global impact beyond the scope of voluntary philanthropy or domestic taxation alone.
3. Hunger and lack of access to clean water remain two of the most solvable human crises, requiring sustainable funding mechanisms commensurate with modern private wealth capacity.
4. American innovation, infrastructure, and markets enable the creation of such wealth; therefore, its highest tiers must contribute proportionally to preserving global life, stability, and dignity.

(b) Purpose:
The purpose of this Act is to:

- Legally require U.S.-based trillionaires to contribute annually to internationally governed food and water security efforts;
- Establish a transparent, auditable mechanism for stewardship accountability;
- Reaffirm the United States' global leadership in humanitarian innovation and responsible capitalism.

SECTION 3. DEFINITIONS
As used in this Act:

1. Trillionaire – A natural person, citizen or legal resident of the United States, whose global net worth equals or exceeds $1,000,000,000,000 USD, as certified annually by the Office of Global Survival Obligations (OGSO).
2. Net Worth – Total verified assets, including publicly and privately held stocks, equity in closely held corporations, real estate, digital assets, offshore holdings, trusts, cash reserves, and intellectual property valuation.
3. Stewardship Contribution – The annual percentage of a trillionaire's net worth, as defined by this Act, required to be remitted to the Humanity Guarantee Fund via OGSO.
4. OGSO – A federally chartered independent commission tasked with enforcement and oversight of all stewardship-related obligations.
5. Noncompliance – Failure to remit required contributions, refusal to verify net worth, or the obstruction of any aspect of OGSO review or international coordination.

SECTION 4. STEWARDSHIP OBLIGATION THRESHOLDS AND FORMULA

(a) Contribution Schedule:

Trillionaire individuals are required to remit annually the following:

- 0.5% of net worth between $1 trillion and $1.2 trillion

- 1.0% of net worth between $1.2 trillion and $1.5 trillion
- 2.5% of any net worth in excess of $1.5 trillion

(b) Contribution Floor and Ceiling:

- The minimum annual contribution may not be less than $5 billion USD.
- The total contribution may not exceed 2.5% of verified net worth without voluntary election or Tribunal penalty.

(c) Indexing for Inflation:
The contribution thresholds will be recalibrated every 5 years by the Secretary of the Treasury, in alignment with the Consumer Price Index (CPI) and global income distribution standards.

SECTION 5. ESTABLISHMENT OF THE OFFICE FOR GLOBAL SURVIVAL OBLIGATIONS (OGSO)

(a) Structure and Authority:

- OGSO shall be established as an independent federal agency with administrative, enforcement, and audit powers.
- OGSO shall be led by a nonpartisan Stewardship Commission, composed of five presidential appointees with staggered ten-year terms, confirmed by the Senate.

(b) Duties:

- Certify and verify net worth of qualifying individuals annually.
- Calculate and collect annual contributions.
- Collaborate with the Department of State, USAID, and treaty-aligned international organizations for disbursement.
- Maintain and publish a real-time Digital Ledger of Stewardship.
- Investigate suspected avoidance, delay, fraud, or interference.

(c) Reporting Requirements:

- OGSO must report annually to Congress on:
    - Funds collected,
    - Impact metrics,
    - Compliance status,
    - Citizen oversight data,
    - Any enforcement proceedings.

SECTION 6. ENFORCEMENT AND PENALTIES

(a) Failure to Report:

- Up to $100 million in fines,
- Compelled financial disclosure through the Department of the Treasury.

(b) Failure to Contribute (Delinquency >180 days):

- Public listing on Stewardship Delinquency Register,

- Freezing of all U.S.-based digital and physical financial accounts,
- Denial of federal licenses, procurement contracts, and market privileges.

(c) Evasion, Fraud, or Willful Misreporting:

- Civil fines up to three times the unpaid contribution,
- Referral to the U.S. Department of Justice for criminal investigation,
- Ineligibility for participation in sovereign investment, defense contracting, or privileged partnerships.

SECTION 7. GLOBAL COORDINATION AND TREATY ALIGNMENT

(a) International Cooperation:

The Secretary of State, in consultation with OGSO and relevant agencies, shall initiate formal alignment of this Act with:

- The United Nations Global Committee for Food and Water Security (GCFWS),
- The World Bank

TRILLIONAIRE ETHICS and the End of Philanthropy Theater

Philanthropy, as it stands, is optional. Tax shelters disguised as "foundations" allow the ultra-wealthy to control what problems are worthy, who gets help, and what counts as "impact."

The Trillionaire Stewardship Act ends this model.

It says:

- The world's greatest needs are not branding opportunities.
- Extreme wealth is not a license — it's a lien.
- The richest people must function like micro-sovereigns — with legal duties, not vibes.

Global justice starts with extreme wealth governance
This act is not about punishment. It is about repair.

It does not begrudge invention, risk, or reward. But it draws a line at the myth that billionaires-turned-trillionaires can operate without checks, responsibilities, or redistribution.

It is a mechanism by which we:

- Fund global post-scarcity transitions
- Enforce the right to food and water
- Break the cycle of extraction without accountability

And in doing so, we make real the declaration so often repeated and so rarely funded:

Human rights are universal — not for sale, not for permission.

What These Acts Share

Each of these legislative models:

- Embraces universality with flexibility — national guarantees shaped by local context.

- Establishes rights-based funding formulas — tying budgets to fulfillment thresholds, not market cycles.
- Prioritizes democratic governance — giving communities control over resource use, planning, and feedback.
- Operates as part of a transition economy — acknowledging the necessary movement away from extraction and toward care, regeneration, and sufficiency.

And each of them represents a structural departure from business-as-usual. No tweaks. No pilot purgatories. Transformation in code and culture.

In the next section, we'll explore how these acts can be seeded locally and municipally — allowing bold ideas to take root where people live, before scaling to the federal level.

Because the best legislation doesn't come from think tanks. It comes from neighborhoods.

Local and State-Level Pilot Legislation and Municipal Adoption Strategies

You don't need to wait for Congress to change the world.

Throughout U.S. history, local and state governments have pioneered some of the nation's most iconic social policies — often years or decades before federal adoption. Social Security, labor protections, environmental laws, and public health initiatives were all tested municipally before becoming national models.

Today, the same is possible for economic rights and post-scarcity systems. Cities, counties, and states can lead the way by launching pilot programs, charter amendments, and shadow governance models that demonstrate what is possible — and shift the Overton window in real time.

Here's how.

1. Home Rule as a Tool for Innovation

Most U.S. cities operate under "home rule" provisions — meaning they can pass local laws so long as they don't conflict with state or federal statutes. While preemption battles are real (particularly in conservative-led states), home rule powers allow municipalities to:

- Set housing, zoning, and rent control policies
- Expand public health, transit, and education services
- Establish worker protections and public benefit guarantees
- Pilot guaranteed income or basic services programs
- Design local economic governance models (e.g., participatory budgeting, public banks)

Municipal governments are also closer to the people, often more nimble, and more open to experimentation than federal agencies.

The result? Cities can act as proof-of-concept incubators — testing radical ideas at human scale.

2. Examples of Local Post-Scarcity Prototypes
  A. Jackson, Mississippi – The Cooperative Economy

- The late Mayor Chokwe Lumumba and his son envisioned a "solidarity economy" built on cooperative ownership, land trusts, and participatory governance.
- Though often blocked by state-level resistance, the vision seeded national discourse around Black-led economic democracy.

B. Stockton, California – Guaranteed Income

- Launched one of the country's first guaranteed income pilots under Mayor Michael Tubbs.
- Results: decreased volatility in employment, improved mental health, and increased full-time job acquisition.

C. Ithaca, New York – Community Currency

- Introduced the Ithaca HOUR to support local economic sovereignty and value exchange beyond corporate pricing structures.

D. Seattle, Washington – Green New Deal Oversight Board

- Created a board of frontline and environmental justice community members to oversee public climate investments, making budgeting democratic and just.

E. Denver, Colorado – Universal Preschool

- Voter-approved public financing guarantees preschool access to all families, improving school readiness and closing opportunity gaps.

These aren't just quirky side projects. They're post-scarcity design in action — reallocating resources, building commons, and shrinking artificial scarcity one neighborhood at a time.

3. Municipal Strategies for Adoption

Cities and states can deploy a range of tools to pilot and implement rights-based policies:

A. Charter Amendments

- Add language guaranteeing housing, healthcare, or food as a right of residency.
- Example: New York City's "Right to Shelter" mandate has existed since 1981.

B. Participatory Budgeting

- Allocate a portion of the city budget (even just 1%) to be planned and decided directly by residents.
- Extend to climate resilience, care infrastructure, or UBS pilots.

C. Municipal Universal Basic Services (UBS) Zones

- Designate neighborhoods to receive bundled access to services: free transit, guaranteed food, housing support, community healthcare.

- Measure impact using SROI and WELLBY indicators.

D. Local Wealth Capture Mechanisms

- Impose progressive municipal wealth taxes, luxury real estate surcharges, or vacancy fees to fund equity programs.
- Reinforce through land use tools like community land trusts or split-rate property tax systems.

E. Data and Dashboard Democratization

- Build public wellbeing dashboards to track housing, health, food access, mental health, and community cohesion — and tie funding to improvements.
- Involve residents in setting indicators, interpreting results, and co-designing responses.

4. State-Level Leverage and Legal Shielding

States with progressive governance (e.g., California, New York, Massachusetts, Oregon, Washington) can:

- Enshrine economic rights in their state constitutions
- Pass statewide UBS packages with opt-in municipal partnerships
- Launch public option programs in housing, healthcare, or broadband

- Create post-scarcity commissions to plan long-term transitions
- Fund local pilot replication grants to support rural and urban communities alike

States can also shield municipalities from preemption — or, in some cases, override regressive federal policy through state-based guarantees.

Example:

California's Medi-Cal system provides health access to undocumented residents, going beyond federal Medicaid eligibility.

5. Networks, Scaling, and Contagious Imagination

The goal of local action is not isolation. It's contagion.

- Cities that implement pilot UBS models can document outcomes and create open-source toolkits.
- Networks like WEGo (Wellbeing Economy Governments) and ICLEI (Local Governments for Sustainability)can help cities collaborate globally.
- Regional compacts (e.g., Pacific Northwest, Rust Belt resilience coalitions) can harmonize planning across borders and political jurisdictions.

In time, enough local wins build federal pressure. As with marriage equality or cannabis decriminalization, what begins as fringe becomes mainstream — because people see, feel, and believe the difference.

. . .

FROM PILOT to Precedent

There's an old organizing phrase: "First they ignore you. Then they laugh at you. Then they fight you. Then you win."

In the language of governance:

First they call it a pilot. Then they call it a program. Then they call it a right.

And once it's a right?

They can't take it back.

In the next section, we'll examine how to rewire federal agencies for human outcomes — turning institutions like the Fed, HHS, and HUD into champions of sufficiency, not scarcity.

Because transformational legislation needs a home — and our current institutions weren't built for the future we're trying to create.

9

REWIRING FEDERAL AGENCIES FOR HUMAN OUTCOMES

Vignette: Evelyn, a USDA Caseworker in Montana
For 22 years, Evelyn Martinez had worked at the USDA field office in Billings, Montana. Her job was technically food assistance, but it often felt more like systemic triage. She processed SNAP benefits, verified documentation, and monitored compliance for food aid across rural counties and tribal lands.

She knew the names of every food pantry manager in a 100-mile radius. She had cried with mothers who couldn't find formula, advocated for seniors who didn't have internet access to complete online applications, and watched more than one cattle rancher walk in for food aid with their hat in hand, ashamed but desperate.

Most days, Evelyn did everything she could — except change the system.

Then the agency's mission changed.

Following the ratification of the 28th Amendment and the passage of the Universal Basic Services Framework Act, the USDA was no longer tasked with managing scarcity. It was now mandated to guarantee nutrition sovereignty as a federally enforceable right.

Her new job? Designing regional food ecosystems with local growers, co-ops, and tribal councils — no more asset tests or emergency stopgaps. Evelyn now oversaw a food commons trust — coordinating regional planning to ensure that everyone within her jurisdiction had year-round access to healthy, culturally appropriate, and sustainably grown food.

She had a new title: Community Nutritional Steward.

She didn't push paper anymore. She co-created resilience.

On a sunny spring morning, Evelyn stood at the opening of a regional food hub in Crow Agency, funded through the Department's new Rural Sovereignty Grant. She handed out seed packets, hugged elders, and smiled at the murals painted by local high school students.

She knew the future of public service wasn't in paperwork. It was in provisioning, partnership, and repair.

And for the first time in two decades, she no longer felt like she was managing poverty.

She was designing sufficiency.

Repurposing the Federal Reserve for Full Employment and Equitable Credit Access

The U.S. Federal Reserve System was created in 1913 to do one thing: stabilize the banking system. Over the last century, its power has expanded far beyond its original scope. Today, it is arguably the most powerful economic institution in the country — influencing employment, wages, interest rates, capital flows, housing markets, global finance, and even climate risk.

Yet for all its influence, the Fed remains structurally unaccountable, politically insulated, and philosophically aligned with scarcity logic. Its primary goal has been to balance "maximum employment" with "price stability" — a vague dual mandate that, in practice, often prioritizes keeping inflation low over getting people employed.

In the era of economic rights and post-scarcity design, this is no longer acceptable.

The Federal Reserve must be rewired to serve not just markets — but people.

1. Why the Fed Needs to Change

Under the current structure, the Federal Reserve:

- Uses interest rate hikes to slow down the economy and "cool" the labor market when inflation rises — effectively increasing unemployment as a policy lever.
- Injects trillions into the financial system via quantitative easing, disproportionately benefiting asset holders while doing little for wage workers or renters.
- Operates with minimal public input — with regional Reserve Bank boards often populated by private-sector executives and devoid of labor, community, or environmental voices.
- Avoids responsibility for credit discrimination, redlining legacies, or racial wealth gaps — even though it has the tools to address them.

This approach reflects a foundational flaw: treating money creation and credit access as neutral tools, rather than political levers that shape who eats, who works, who builds, and who gets to dream.

. . .

2. A New Mandate: From Price Stability to People Stability

The post-scarcity transformation begins by rewriting the Federal Reserve Act — expanding and clarifying the Fed's legal mission to include:

- Full Employment as a Constitutional Right
- The Fed must use all tools to maintain true full employment — defined not by labor market tightness, but by universal access to dignified, voluntary, and meaningful work.
- Equitable Credit Access
- The Fed must ensure all communities — especially historically excluded ones — have access to low-interest, mission-driven credit for housing, business creation, and local infrastructure.
- Sustainability and Just Transition Financing
- The Fed must prioritize green investment mandates and climate risk mitigation — ensuring that money creation supports planetary stability, not extraction.
- Anti-Extractive Capital Stewardship
- The Fed should actively discourage speculative finance, offshore hoarding, and shareholder-first practices — and favor capital allocation that serves public outcomes.

This new mandate would be legally enforceable, subject to annual public rights performance audits, and co-governed with input from marginalized and working-class communities.

. . .

3. Tools for Democratic Monetary Policy

To meet this expanded mandate, the Fed must adopt new tools:

A. Dual Interest Rates for Social Impact

- Offer lower interest rates to institutions investing in:
  - Affordable housing
  - Worker-owned cooperatives
  - Regenerative agriculture
  - Public infrastructure
- Raise rates for speculative, extractive, or high-risk financial activities.

B. Community Credit Facilities

- Establish regional Public Credit Facilities under Reserve Banks, issuing:
  - Low-interest loans to municipal governments
  - Start-up capital for social enterprises
  - Climate adaptation bonds
- Operate in partnership with postal banking, CDFIs, and state banks.

C. Full Employment Guarantee via Public Jobs Program

- Create a federally backed job guarantee in coordination with the Department of Labor and Department of Economic Rights.
- Use Fed financing to support local governments and NGOs hiring for:
  - Care work
  - Climate resilience
  - Public arts and education
  - Housing retrofits

The goal: no one unemployed involuntarily, ever again.

D. Digital Commons Currency (Optional Track)

- Explore a publicly governed digital dollar for direct economic provisioning — enabling universal basic services payments, time-banking, or mutual aid coordination with zero transaction fees and full privacy protections.

4. Structural Reform: Democratizing the Fed

To make these changes permanent, the Fed's governance must also change.

Key proposals:

- Board of Governors Reform: Require seats for labor unions, environmental justice advocates, Indigenous economic leaders, and public health economists.
- Regional Bank Board Overhaul: Replace corporate-dominated advisory roles with representatives from community development

organizations, racial justice networks, and rural/urban mutual aid groups.
- Transparency Requirements: All decisions and modeling assumptions must be published in open, accessible formats with public comment periods and participatory oversight.

The Fed must no longer be a fortress of elite consensus. It must be an engine of public sufficiency, legally bound to fulfill the 28th Amendment's economic guarantees.

5. International Coordination

The U.S. dollar is a global reserve currency. Fed decisions ripple across the world — impacting debt burdens in the Global South, trade balances, and development financing.

A post-scarcity-aligned Fed would:

- Coordinate with the IMF, World Bank, and BRICS+ nations to de-dollarize risk and increase Special Drawing Rights for public provisioning worldwide.
- Support the Trillionaire Stewardship Act by conditioning financial services access on compliance with global food and water goals.
- Create a Global Public Investment Clearinghouse to align sovereign wealth funds and development banks with planetary wellbeing metrics.

FROM CENTRAL BANKING to Common Stewardship
What if the Fed saw itself not as the babysitter of inflation, but as the guardian of sufficiency?
What if its success wasn't judged by Dow Jones upticks — but by:

- Declines in homelessness
- Increases in cooperative ownership
- Universal access to clean water, food, and shelter

This is not just possible. It is necessary.

Because a post-scarcity world cannot be built on a monetary system designed to maintain structural unemployment and perpetual extraction.

It must be built on finance that serves life — not leverage.

In the next section, we'll examine how to repurpose other federal agencies — including HHS, HUD, and USDA — from scarcity managers into abundance engineers.

Because every institution, not just the Fed, must now be measured by a single question:

Did it help people thrive — or did it protect a system where only some could?

Repurposing HHS, HUD, and USDA from Scarcity Management to Abundance Engineering

Federal social agencies are some of the largest employers and budget administrators in the U.S. government — yet they've often been forced to operate under a scarcity paradigm: rationing help, administering austerity, and enforcing eligibility rules that exclude far more than they serve.

In the wake of a new constitutional mandate for economic rights, agencies like Health and Human Services

(HHS), Housing and Urban Development (HUD), and the Department of Agriculture (USDA) must evolve from fragmented, means-tested bureaucracy into bold platforms of provisioning — guaranteeing universal access to core rights and serving as the backbone of post-scarcity governance.

Let's examine each one in turn.

1. HHS – From Payer of Last Resort to Steward of Universal Wellbeing

The Department of Health and Human Services is the largest civilian federal agency, overseeing programs like:

- Medicare and Medicaid
- TANF and CHIP
- Head Start
- SAMHSA (mental health services)
- The CDC and NIH

Historically, HHS has operated as a fragmented responder — a manager of crises, administrator of subsidies, and payer of last resort for the uninsured.

In a post-scarcity model, HHS becomes the national anchor of a universal care system.

Key Transformations:

- Administer Medicare for All: Consolidate all federal health programs into a single-payer system covering all residents — regardless of age, income, or employment.
- Universal Mental Health Infrastructure: Scale SAMHSA into a national public mental health

system, including school-based care, trauma-informed workplaces, and community crisis response units that replace carceral mental health interventions.
- National Caregiver Corps: Create a federally supported job guarantee for home health aides, elder caregivers, and community health workers — with union wages and public pensions.
- Preventive Health Equity Index: Shift budgeting toward upstream interventions (air quality, nutrition, mobility) and tie funding to reductions in chronic disease, health disparities, and toxic stress.

Goal: No one dies from preventable illness. No one goes bankrupt from a hospital visit. Health is assumed, not earned.

2. HUD – From Managing Poverty Housing to Guaranteeing Shelter as Infrastructure

The Department of Housing and Urban Development has long been underfunded, overburdened, and structurally boxed in by a real estate market that treats shelter as a speculative asset.

Public housing has been stigmatized. Vouchers are insufficient. Rental subsidies are deeply bureaucratic. And homeownership, the so-called "American Dream," remains a racially and generationally segregated privilege.

In a post-scarcity paradigm, HUD becomes the national housing infrastructure agency — guaranteeing shelter the way the Department of Transportation guarantees roads.

Key Transformations:

- Universal Housing Guarantee: Phase out vouchers in favor of direct public housing provisioning, housing-first models, and community land trusts.
- Green Building and Retrofit Mandate: Oversee the decarbonization and climate-proofing of all publicly supported housing stock.
- Housing as a Commons Platform: Provide technical assistance and capital grants for cooperative housing, social housing, and Indigenous land reclamation.
- Eviction Abolition Act: Replace eviction court systems with mediation and housing stabilization boards focused on keeping people housed, not punishing poverty.

Goal: Housing becomes a pillar of public infrastructure — like water, electricity, or roads. No one lives on the street. No one is rent-burdened. Shelter is not conditional.

3. USDA – From Subsidizing Agribusiness to Coordinating Food Sovereignty

The U.S. Department of Agriculture, while historically tasked with food assistance and farming policy, has been dominated by industrial agriculture interests — often subsidizing monocrops, supporting chemical-intensive farming, and regulating nutrition through a lens of cost-efficiency rather than nutritional justice.

In a rights-based economy, USDA shifts from supporting profit agriculture to coordinating local, regenerative, and dignified food systems for all.

Key Transformations:

- Universal Nutrition Guarantee: Replace SNAP with a guaranteed right to food — through a hybrid of free community kitchens, school meals, urban farms, and dignified food credits redeemable in all stores.
- Department of Food Sovereignty: Integrate tribal, regional, and agroecological councils into USDA policy planning. Ensure that food is culturally appropriate, ecologically sound, and locally grown.
- Land Access Reparations Act: Launch a national program for land back, BIPOC farm ownership, and intergenerational land restoration — funded through land value taxation and corporate agriculture divestment.
- Decentralized Food Hubs: Invest in cooperative processing, cold storage, seed banks, and mutual aid food logistics — eliminating long, brittle, fossil-fueled supply chains.

Goal: Everyone eats. Everyone eats well. Food is a right, not a transaction.

A New Culture of Governance

The transformation of these agencies requires more than new mandates — it requires a new internal culture:

- Workers are trained as public stewards, not gatekeepers.
- Communities are viewed as partners, not clients.

- Budgets are designed with Social Return on Investment (SROI) metrics.
- Metrics of success shift from service "efficiency" to lived dignity.

Imagine a USDA regional director who sees their job not as cutting SNAP fraud, but as ensuring no child goes to school hungry.

Imagine an HHS staffer tasked not with insurance auditing, but with eliminating preventable deaths in their county.

Imagine a HUD analyst tracking time-to-housing after displacement as their key performance indicator.

This is governance for sufficiency.

This is abundance engineering.

In the next section, we'll explore how to leverage the Defense Production Act — long used for war mobilization — to accelerate peaceful transitions toward climate resilience, food security, and economic rights fulfillment.

Because if we can build bombs on demand, we can build sufficiency by design.

Using the Defense Production Act for Peacetime Sustainability Transitions

In moments of national crisis, governments don't ask the market for permission — they command production. They mobilize resources. They coordinate logistics. They prioritize people over profits. And they do it fast.

In the United States, the legal backbone for this capacity is the Defense Production Act of 1950 (DPA) — a law originally enacted during the Korean War, but used extensively during World War II through predecessor authorities to transform the U.S. economy into an all-hands-on-deck wartime machine.

What's often forgotten — or deliberately obscured — is that the DPA still exists today. It has been invoked to:

- Prioritize vaccine and PPE production during the COVID-19 pandemic
- Accelerate baby formula manufacturing during domestic shortages
- Support energy grid repair in Puerto Rico
- Speed up semiconductor production and lithium battery supply chains

But here's the thing:

If we can use the DPA to build missiles and mend supply chains,

we can use it to guarantee housing, decarbonize infrastructure, and feed everyone.

It's time to expand and reframe the DPA as a constitutional tool for post-scarcity and economic rights provisioning.

1. What the DPA Actually Allows

The Defense Production Act grants the President wide-ranging powers to:

- Direct private industry to prioritize federal contracts
- Allocate materials, services, and facilities to national defense needs
- Incentivize expansion of production capacity
- Create loan guarantees and direct purchases
- Control price, distribution, and rationing of critical goods

Crucially, the term "national defense" has been interpreted broadly — encompassing homeland security, energy resilience, and now, arguably, economic and environmental survival.

What's missing is the political will to treat climate collapse, housing precarity, and systemic hunger as national emergencies on par with war.

2. Reframing the DPA: From Militarism to Mutualism

A post-scarcity reinterpretation of the DPA would:

- Expand "national defense" to include:
    - Universal housing and food security
    - Climate adaptation and decarbonization
    - Care infrastructure and public health
    - Renewable energy sovereignty
    - Digital and knowledge commons development
- Establish a permanent Peacetime Mobilization Authority (PMA) within the Executive Office of the President, tasked with:
    - Identifying rights-fulfillment infrastructure shortfalls
    - Coordinating cross-agency DPA deployment
    - Partnering with municipal and state governments for rapid scaling

This is not new legislation — it is existing power waiting to be re-aimed.

3. Key Areas for DPA-Driven Post-Scarcity Investment

A. Housing Buildout and Retrofit

- Mandate production of modular, zero-carbon housing units using U.S.-sourced materials.
- Coordinate with HUD and labor unions to retrofit all public housing for energy efficiency and climate resilience.
- Create mobile shelter fabrication hubs for disaster-impacted and displaced populations.

B. Regenerative Food Systems

- Fund localized food production: vertical farms, school gardens, agroforestry, Indigenous stewardship zones.
- Mandate prioritized contracts for soil-restorative agriculture tools, seed banks, and water capture systems.

C. Renewable Energy and Storage

- Mass-produce and deploy community-scale solar and battery systems, prioritizing frontline and rural areas.
- Fund manufacturing cooperatives for heat pumps, induction stoves, electric transit fleets, and energy microgrids.

D. Health and Care Infrastructure

- Expand PPE, ventilation, and pharmaceutical sovereignty for chronic and infectious health security.

- Build care cooperatives and neighborhood health pods, particularly in underserved rural and urban zones.

E. Public Information and Digital Access

- Require expansion of free, encrypted, high-speed broadband and eliminate monopolistic barriers to digital infrastructure.
- Deploy secure public cloud infrastructure and open-source platforms for education, governance, and civic coordination.

4. Integrating DPA with Economic Rights Enforcement

To prevent the DPA from being used to simply pad private profit margins (as often occurs), it must be:

- Tied to rights-based outcomes: e.g., "X housing units per 1,000 residents," "Y% reduction in food insecurity," "Z gigawatts of energy per region."
- Subject to community governance and consent: local councils decide implementation priorities and labor standards.
- Aligned with The Trillionaire Stewardship Act: those with wealth beyond the $1T threshold fund infrastructure buildouts where shortfalls persist.

The DPA becomes not just a law — but a lever of global responsibility.

. . .

5. Creating a Culture of Peacetime Production
   Imagine:

   - A peacetime industrial strategy centered not on GDP growth, but wellbeing metrics
   - Engineers designing public goods, not weapons
   - Federal funding tied to ecosystem restoration, not extractive ROI
   - The nation mobilized not against an enemy — but for each other

This isn't nostalgia for the New Deal. It's a new design for the common era — built on existing power, reimagined for new priorities.

Because we already know how to build at scale, fast, and together.

We've just never done it for sufficiency — only for war.

It's time to redirect the arsenal of democracy toward the architecture of dignity.

In the next chapter, we turn from the national to the international — beginning with a global call for a New Universal Declaration of Economic Rights, and how the United Nations can integrate post-scarcity principles into binding global law.

Because economic rights should stop at no border — and dignity is not a domestic product.

10

A UPDATED UNIVERSAL DECLARATION OF ECONOMIC RIGHTS

Vignette: Amara, a High School Teacher in Lagos

Amara stood at the front of her overcrowded classroom, trying to quiet the students as the ceiling fans groaned against the heat. Thirty-eight teenagers sat shoulder to shoulder, sharing tattered textbooks and sweating through their uniforms. Some hadn't eaten since the day before.

She had taught history for eleven years — long enough to remember when the government promised education for all. But year after year, the budgets shrank while foreign investors raked in profits from Nigeria's energy exports. Amara's salary barely covered transportation and food for her two daughters. When her youngest was hospitalized with an asthma attack, the clinic demanded payment upfront. She borrowed money from five coworkers.

One evening, as she prepped lessons by candlelight during a blackout, her eldest daughter brought her a printout from the school printer — a translation of a proposed updated Universal Declaration of Economic Rights being circulated online.

Amara read it out loud:

"Every human being has the right to live free from hunger, homelessness, and humiliation. To have shelter, nourishment, education, and medical care not as a privilege, but as a birthright of being alive."

She set the paper down.

"If they mean it," she said softly, "this changes everything."

Why an updated Universal Declaration Is Necessary

The Universal Declaration of Human Rights (UDHR) was adopted in 1948 — a milestone moment in global history. But despite its moral force, the UDHR has always had a fundamental imbalance:

- Civil and political rights (speech, assembly, due process) are widely enforced.
- Economic and social rights (food, housing, education, healthcare) remain aspirational — honored more in principle than practice.

The International Covenant on Economic, Social and Cultural Rights (ICESCR) was meant to fix this. Yet the United States never ratified it, and many signatories underfund its obligations. Economic rights remain non-justiciable in most countries — meaning people can't sue to enforce them.

This legal inequality reflects a philosophical one:

- Political rights are treated as freedom from interference
- Economic rights are seen as asks for generosity

But in a post-scarcity framework, this dichotomy dissolves.

There is no freedom when people are hungry.

No dignity in being homeless.

No democracy in an empty stomach.

The updated Universal Declaration of Economic Rights begins by correcting this imbalance — codifying sufficiency as a legal, enforceable, and universal human right.

Key Articles in the Declaration

The proposed updated Universal Declaration of Economic Rights contains 12 core articles. Here are foundational examples:

Article 1 – Right to Sufficient Nourishment

Every person has the right to access sufficient, nutritious, and culturally appropriate food on a daily basis. Governments must guarantee this right through public infrastructure, sustainable agriculture, and emergency provision mechanisms.

Article 2 – Right to Safe and Secure Housing

Every person has the right to dignified, stable, and habitable shelter that ensures personal security, health, and privacy. Eviction without cause or access to adequate alternatives is a violation of this right.

Article 3 – Right to Universal Healthcare

Every person has the right to timely, quality, and comprehensive healthcare regardless of income, age, employment status, or geographic location. This includes mental health services and preventive care.

Article 4 – Right to Education and Lifelong Learning

All individuals have the right to free and accessible

education from early childhood through secondary schooling, with access to higher education and vocational training based on capacity and desire, not wealth.

Article 5 – Right to Clean Water and Sanitation

Every person has the right to affordable, safe, and continuous access to clean drinking water and hygienic sanitation facilities, recognizing water as a shared and sacred commons.

Article 6 – Right to Sustainable Energy

Every person has the right to reliable, affordable, and sustainable energy sufficient to meet basic household, health, and informational needs. This includes electricity and clean cooking fuel.

Article 7 – Right to Digital Access

Every person has the right to access the internet and digital infrastructure necessary to participate fully in modern economic, civic, and educational life. Digital exclusion is a form of systemic inequality.

Article 8 – Right to Income Security and Meaningful Work

Every person has the right to sufficient income to meet basic needs through access to fair wages, dignified work, or guaranteed public income support, such as universal basic income or equivalent social protections.

Article 9 – Right to Rest and Leisure

Every person has the right to rest, leisure, and regular periods of paid time off, recognizing that human dignity includes freedom from constant economic pressure and exploitation.

Article 10 – Right to Environmental Health and Resilience

Every person has the right to live in a clean, safe, and

ecologically balanced environment. Economic systems must be governed by principles of sustainability, stewardship, and intergenerational equity.

Article 11 – Right to Public Goods and Commons

All people have a right to equitable participation in and benefit from public goods, including transportation, parks, libraries, community spaces, and cultural resources, without discrimination.

Article 12 – Right to Democratic Economic Participation

Every person has the right to participate in decisions that shape the economic systems they live under, including workplace democracy, cooperative ownership models, and participatory budgeting at local and national levels.

These rights are non-hierarchical and mutually reinforcing — recognizing that economic and ecological systems are interdependent and must be governed accordingly.

Implementation Mechanisms

The updated Universal Declaration of Economic Rights isn't meant to be symbolic. It's built for enforcement.

A. Treaty Integration

- Countries ratify the Declaration through the UN, triggering automatic alignment with national constitutions and development plans.
- States must publish national sufficiency indices to track compliance.

B. International Economic Rights Council (IERC)

- A new UN body tasked with:

- Monitoring violations (like the Human Rights Council)
- Issuing public censure and sanctions
- Coordinating with regional courts and civil society watchdogs

C. Citizen Legal Standing

- Individuals or communities can file economic rights complaints directly to the IERC or national ombudsman offices.
- Collective rights suits can compel governments to allocate budgets or revise austerity policies.

D. Global Compliance Fund

- Funded through:
    - Proportional contributions from member states (based on GDP)
    - Trillionaire Stewardship Act obligations
    - Ethical wealth taxes on transnational corporations
- Supports states that demonstrate need and participatory implementation plans.

Strategic Alignment with Existing Frameworks

To avoid bureaucratic duplication, the Declaration is woven into existing global tools:

- Aligned with SDGs, but backed by enforcement
- Integrated with Universal Periodic Review cycles

- Paired with new Economic Justice Indicators, like WELLBYs and SROI metrics
- Modeled on successful precedents, like CEDAW, CRPD, and ICESCR, but updated for the digital and ecological age

It also supports regional adaptation — allowing countries to localize implementation according to Indigenous, Afrodescendant, and ecological traditions.

Why Now?

Because the stakes couldn't be higher:

- Billionaires add $2 billion to their fortunes daily while 800 million go to bed hungry.
- Climate change threatens every pillar of economic life — from food systems to habitability.
- Authoritarianism feeds off economic insecurity.

The updated Universal Declaration of Economic Rights is not a wish list. It is a necessary contract for global survival.

In a world of plenty, deprivation is not misfortune — it is policy.

And policy can change.

The Third Covenant – Economic Dignity Alongside Civil and Political Rights

In the architecture of modern human rights, two legal pillars stand tall:

1. The International Covenant on Civil and Political Rights (ICCPR)
2. The International Covenant on Economic, Social, and Cultural Rights (ICESCR)

Both were adopted in 1966, two decades after the Universal Declaration of Human Rights. Together, they form the International Bill of Human Rights — a dual commitment to liberty and livelihood.

But in practice, the system is lopsided.

- The ICCPR is widely ratified and actively enforced. It covers freedom of speech, religion, due process, voting, and personal safety. Countries can be sued, sanctioned, or condemned for violations.
- The ICESCR, while equally sweeping — covering education, work, health, housing, and cultural life — is often treated as a soft guideline, with no binding enforcement mechanisms, no global court, and no real teeth.

The result?

Civil and political rights are treated as immediate and inviolable, while economic rights are aspirational — something to get to *later*, when convenient, when affordable, when politically palatable.

This is not just an oversight. It's an ideological artifact of a world order built on market fundamentalism, neocolonial resource control, and a convenient belief that economic dignity is optional.

But in the 21st century, that framework no longer holds.

- Climate change, pandemic recovery, and wealth inequality are not threats to civil liberty alone — they are threats to life itself.
- The idea of a human right that does not include shelter, sustenance, and safety is not liberalism — it's abandonment.

Hence the call for a Third Covenant: a binding, enforceable, and globally ratified treaty that elevates economic rights to the level of political rights — with equal legal force and institutional protection.

What Is the Third Covenant?

The Third Covenant would function as a stand-alone international treaty, yet also serve as the completion of the original human rights vision:

- It would make material sufficiency — housing, food, water, healthcare, education, and livelihood — legally guaranteed under international law.
- It would create obligations, not suggestions: timelines for fulfillment, minimum budget thresholds, redress pathways for violations.
- It would require constitutional alignment at the national level — similar to how ICCPR and CEDAW triggered law reforms around due process and gender equity.

And it would merge modern realities — digital rights, ecological dignity, care work, and economic participation — into the legal lexicon of rights-based governance.

. . .

CORE PROVISIONS **of the Third Covenant**
The Third Covenant would include binding articles on:
A. Universal Material Guarantees
Every person has the right to:

- Adequate housing and protection from eviction
- Nutritious, culturally appropriate food
- Safe drinking water and sanitation
- Accessible, preventative, and emergency healthcare
- Free and quality public education
- Income security or guaranteed dignified employment

B. Ecological and Temporal Security
All individuals and communities have the right to:

- Clean air, a stable climate, and restoration of degraded ecosystems
- Time for rest, care, family, and cultural life without economic penalty
- Protection from economic displacement due to automation, crisis, or colonization

C. Participatory Economic Governance
People have the right to:

- Participate in budgetary, planning, and resource allocation processes
- Form worker and tenant cooperatives without corporate retaliation
- Access data, digital tools, and financial

infrastructure necessary to exercise economic citizenship

Enforcement Architecture

To give the Covenant power, it must have legal mechanisms and political incentives:

A. International Economic Rights Court (IERC)

- Modeled on the International Criminal Court and European Court of Human Rights
- Hears cases from individuals, civil society, or states
- Issues binding rulings, sanctions, and orders for remediation

B. Rights-Based Budget Review

- Countries must submit annual reports showing alignment of national budgets with economic rights benchmarks (e.g., % GDP spent on housing, education, care).
- Independent panels evaluate and publish compliance scores.

C. Redress and Reparations Fund

- Supported by contributions from high-income nations, the IMF, and The Trillionaire Stewardship Fund
- Provides direct financial support for countries pursuing rapid economic rights implementation

. . .

POLITICAL AND STRATEGIC Pathways

Passing a Third Covenant will not be easy — but it is legally plausible and politically urgent.

Strategic steps include:

- Launching a UN High-Level Panel on Economic Rights Integration (modeled on the Paris Agreement drafting process)
- Mobilizing civil society coalitions across the Global South and Global North — emphasizing that austerity is a shared wound
- Engaging faith traditions, labor unions, and care economies — centering dignity in economic discourse
- Using strategic litigation to build precedent even before full ratification

WHY IT MATTERS NOW

A Third Covenant answers the defining question of our time:

Can we call ourselves a civilized world if we accept starvation, homelessness, and medical abandonment while trillion-dollar fortunes remain untaxed?

It says no.

It recognizes that dignity is indivisible.

And it fulfills the unfinished promise of 1948 — when the Universal Declaration declared rights that still do not govern the world we live in.

With the Third Covenant, we choose to finish what we

started — and build a world where freedom is not theoretical, but tangible.
Where liberty comes with lunch.
And democracy comes with dinner.

Legal Framework for Post-Scarcity Rights in Global Treaties

The promise of universal economic rights cannot be fulfilled through rhetoric alone. For rights to be protected, enforced, and resourced globally, they must be codified in law — not just domestically, but in binding international treaties that hold states accountable across borders and generations.

A post-scarcity world demands a legal infrastructure as resilient, enforceable, and far-reaching as the challenges it aims to address. That infrastructure already exists in part — through a lattice of UN declarations, human rights covenants, environmental compacts, and regional charters. But what we need now is a coherent legal framework that weaves these elements into a unified doctrine of economic dignity, planetary sufficiency, and collective obligation.

This is the legal architecture of the New Universal Declaration of Economic Rights.

1. Three Paths to Legalization of Post-Scarcity Rights
There are three primary mechanisms by which new economic rights can be embedded into global legal systems:
A. Treaty Adoption and Ratification (Multilateral Route)

- Draft and negotiate a new, binding multilateral treaty through the United Nations — modeled

on the ICCPR or ICESCR, but modernized for post-scarcity guarantees.
- The treaty would enter into force upon ratification by a minimum number of states (e.g., 60).
- Signatories would be required to incorporate treaty provisions into domestic legislation and constitutional reforms.
- Key rights would include:
  - Guaranteed housing and shelter access
  - Free, universal public healthcare
  - Universal nutritious food provisioning
  - Ecological stability and reparative environmental justice
  - Income security or work guarantees
  - Right to care and time autonomy

This "Third Covenant" structure would explicitly elevate economic rights to equal standing with civil and political rights under international law.

B. Protocol Expansion to Existing Treaties

- Attach a new Protocol on Economic Sufficiency to the ICESCR or UN Framework Convention on Climate Change (UNFCCC).
- This protocol would outline specific state obligations, implementation timelines, and global funding mechanisms for post-scarcity transition.
- Include:
  - Required % of GDP for economic rights fulfillment

- National dashboards with wellbeing metrics
- Provisions for public complaint mechanisms
- Enforcement through global development finance conditions

This model is faster to negotiate and more politically palatable in the short term, especially if framed as an update rather than a rewrite.

C. Regional Economic Rights Compacts

- Groups of countries (e.g., the African Union, Mercosur, CARICOM, ASEAN, or the EU) enter into binding regional agreements on the right to sufficiency.
- These compacts act as pilot jurisdictions, showing feasibility and impact.
- Examples include:
  - The Right to Food and Clean Water Charter (Africa)
  - The Ecological Housing Guarantee Pact (Europe)
  - The Basic Services for All Treaty (South America)

Over time, these regional agreements can be consolidated into a global harmonized treaty, using the principle of "progressive realization" embedded in ICESCR.

2. Institutional and Judicial Support Mechanisms

Embedding economic rights into global treaties also requires building the institutions to protect them.

A. Global Economic Rights Tribunal (GERT)

- A quasi-judicial body empowered to hear complaints, issue rulings, and recommend enforcement actions related to treaty violations.
- Operates similarly to the Inter-American Court of Human Rights or the African Court on Human and Peoples' Rights.
- Individuals, organizations, and states may submit cases involving:
    - Forced evictions
    - Food system collapse due to corruption or extraction
    - Systemic healthcare exclusion
    - Negligent climate inaction causing economic right violations

B. UN Special Rapporteur on Economic Dignity

- Appointed to monitor and report on compliance with economic rights treaties.
- Publishes annual Global Sufficiency Reports.
- Coordinates with existing treaty bodies and the Office of the High Commissioner for Human Rights (OHCHR).

C. International Development Rights Registry

- Tracks national progress toward economic rights benchmarks (e.g., housing availability per capita, access to clean energy, food security ratings).
- Enables equitable international funding flows —

prioritizing countries demonstrating community-led, transparent implementation.

3. Integrating with Development Finance and Global Aid

To ensure these rights are funded and not just declared, the treaty framework must:

- Embed post-scarcity rights into IMF and World Bank lending conditions
- Require development assistance to support rights-based services, not extractive growth models
- Empower Global South countries to condition trade and investment agreements on economic rights compliance

This aligns directly with:

- The Trillionaire Stewardship Act, which channels wealth into rights infrastructure
- Climate finance mechanisms like Loss and Damage funds and Just Transition strategies
- Sovereign debt restructuring frameworks that prioritize human rights over bondholder profits

4. Legal Standing and Citizen Recourse

Crucially, treaties must provide direct recourse for citizens:

- Individuals and collectives gain legal standing to bring violations to:
    - National courts (which must adopt economic rights enforcement provisions)
    - Regional human rights bodies
    - International Economic Rights Tribunal
- Civil society organizations may submit shadow reports detailing rights violations, triggering international inquiries or sanctions.
- Refugee and migrant protections expand to include economic displacement, allowing those displaced by poverty, hunger, or climate collapse to seek status and redress under post-scarcity rights law.

5. Legal Fusion: Rights for the Future

A legal framework for post-scarcity rights isn't just about solving today's problems — it's about institutionalizing sufficiency for generations to come.

Imagine:

- Constitutions amended worldwide to include the right to clean water, time to care, and food without stigma.
- Climate reparations legally mandated, with quarterly payouts structured like universal dividends.
- Trillion-dollar sovereign wealth funds indexed to wellbeing, not GDP or oil futures.

This legal framework gives us the tools not just to respond to emergencies, but to design systems that prevent them.

It fuses:

- Human rights law
- Ecological stewardship
- Post-growth economics
- And planetary governance

Into a single operating system: one where justice lives in institutions, not just ideals.

Roles for OHCHR, UNDP, and Regional Human Rights Courts

Embedding economic rights into a binding international declaration is only the first step. For these rights to be actionable, measurable, and enforceable, they must be housed within credible institutions with both legal authority and developmental capacity.

This section explores how existing bodies — including the OHCHR, UNDP, and regional human rights courts — can be reoriented and strengthened to become pillars of post-scarcity governance.

Together, they form the global scaffolding of sufficiency — where human rights aren't just monitored, but meaningfully implemented.

1. The Office of the High Commissioner for Human Rights (OHCHR)

Mandate Expansion: From Advocacy to Oversight

The OHCHR has traditionally focused on civil and political rights, supporting country-level human rights offices and reviewing state reports under the Universal Periodic Review (UPR) process. Economic, social, and cultural rights have often been treated as secondary or advisory.

In a post-scarcity framework, OHCHR's mandate must be structurally updated to reflect the centrality of economic dignity as a core human right.

Key Transformations:

- Create a Division of Economic and Ecological Rights (DEER) to house specialized teams in:
    - Housing, nutrition, and health rights
    - Economic participation and care economy
    - Climate and environmental justice as economic rights
- Revise UPR indicators to include national performance on sufficiency metrics, such as:
    - % of population with secure housing
    - Access to clean drinking water
    - School meal and healthcare coverage rates
    - Ecological footprint per capita vs. regeneration rates
- Appoint a High-Level Rapporteur on Post-Scarcity Implementation, tasked with tracking global compliance with the New Universal Declaration.

Strategic Role:

OHCHR becomes the moral anchor and legal watchdog for the Third Covenant — ensuring that no country can claim human rights legitimacy while failing to provide food, shelter, or healthcare.

. . .

2. The United Nations Development Program (UNDP)
Implementation Hub: From Poverty Alleviation to Rights Fulfillment

The UNDP has long worked on sustainable development, capacity building, and poverty reduction, but its frameworks have often reflected neoliberal paradigms — relying heavily on growth metrics, private-sector partnerships, and donor-driven priorities.

A post-scarcity approach requires a reorientation of UNDP from project-based development aid to a guarantor of sufficiency systems.

Key Transformations:

- Align UNDP programming with the 12 Rights of Sufficiency, ensuring all technical assistance and funding advances:
    - Universal basic services
    - Social protection floors
    - Regenerative economies
    - Community sovereignty and governance participation
- Launch a Global Sufficiency Accelerator Program (GSAP) to support countries in building:
    - Housing-first infrastructure
    - Public health and nutrition systems
    - Cooperative ownership models
    - Renewable energy commons
- Replace GDP-focused benchmarks with:
    - Wellbeing-adjusted national accounting
    - Social Return on Investment (SROI) indicators
    - Planetary boundary and ecological integrity thresholds

Strategic Role:
UNDP becomes the technical enabler and funding integrator of post-scarcity transitions — delivering the "how" behind the rights promised in the global treaty.

3. Regional Human Rights Courts
Legal Enforcement: From Civil Adjudication to Economic Justice

Regional courts — including the Inter-American Court of Human Rights, the African Court on Human and Peoples' Rights, and the European Court of Human Rights — have long been key enforcers of human rights within their jurisdictions. In recent years, some have begun ruling on economic and social rights, especially in landmark cases related to housing, water, and health.

These courts are ideally positioned to serve as early enforcers of post-scarcity legal standards.

Key Transformations:

- Incorporate the Third Covenant into regional treaties and charters as a legally binding supplement.
- Expand justiciability of economic rights, ensuring individuals and communities can:
  - File claims against housing exclusion or healthcare denial
  - Sue governments for failing to meet economic rights benchmarks
  - Challenge austerity programs that violate sufficiency obligations
- Create Economic Rights Chambers within each

court to hear high-priority cases, supported by economic and ecological expert panels.
- Allow for amicus briefs and people's tribunals to inform decisions with participatory data and lived experience.

Precedent Examples:

- *Inter-American Court*: Found Colombia guilty of violating the right to water access in Indigenous Wayuu communities.
- *European Court*: Ruled against Hungary for criminalizing homelessness as a violation of human dignity.
- *African Commission*: Issued rulings on forced evictions, land rights, and food sovereignty.

Strategic Role:
Regional courts serve as judicial anchors, ensuring that post-scarcity rights have teeth — and that states are held accountable not just politically, but legally.

4. Coordinated Multilateral Mechanism

To integrate these roles, a Global Economic Rights Implementation Council (GERIC) can be established, co-hosted by OHCHR and UNDP, with seats for:

- Regional court representatives
- UN Special Rapporteurs
- Civil society coalitions and Indigenous councils
- States party to the Third Covenant

- Trillionaire Club delegates with compliance duties under global stewardship law

Mandate:

- Coordinate treaty monitoring and implementation
- Oversee global sufficiency reporting
- Manage complaints and referrals between agencies
- Align multilateral funding flows with rights-based governance

From Institutions of Aid to Instruments of Obligation

For decades, global governance has operated under an asymmetry:

- The Global North writes checks and conditions
- The Global South absorbs impacts and austerity

A post-scarcity treaty flips that structure:

- It binds all countries to universal obligations
- It makes sufficiency a legal minimum, not an aspirational ceiling
- And it transforms aid into a shared duty of repair

Rights are not fulfilled by charity.

They are fulfilled by design — through law, funding, and accountability.

In the next chapter, we move into the financial realm —

beginning with reform of the IMF, World Bank, and global taxation systems to align money with justice and make rights non-negotiable.

Because the future won't be built by declarations alone — it will be built by institutions willing to make them real.

11

GLOBAL FINANCIAL SYSTEM REFORM

Vignette: Raj, a Debt Negotiator in Sri Lanka
Raj adjusted his tie as he stepped into the conference room in Washington, D.C. It was his fourth trip in six months — each one more desperate than the last. Representing Sri Lanka's Ministry of Finance, he was here to renegotiate terms on a $4.5 billion debt package owed to the IMF and foreign bondholders.

Last year, his country had defaulted for the first time in its history. Prices of rice and fuel had skyrocketed. Hospitals rationed medicine. Teachers went unpaid. Families cooked by candlelight. And still, the creditors demanded austerity.

Cut subsidies. Raise taxes. Privatize water. Close public clinics. "Fiscal discipline," they called it.

Raj had spent his career working within the system. He believed in data, in diplomacy, in the promise that cooperation would eventually lead to progress. But now, he felt like a man holding a ledger in a burning house.

That morning, he received a confidential draft from a colleague in Geneva — part of a growing coalition of Global South economists.

It was titled: "The New Bretton Woods Accord for Economic and Ecological Rights."

"*No country should be forced to sacrifice nutrition, shelter, or medical care to pay creditors. Debt repayment cannot supersede human rights. Financial sovereignty is a condition of dignity.*"

Raj read it three times.

He stood up, folded the document into his briefcase, and walked toward the meeting.

This time, he would not ask for leniency.

He would demand justice.

IMF/World Bank Reform – Sovereignty, Conditionality, and Ethical Lending

Few institutions have shaped the modern global economy more than the International Monetary Fund (IMF) and the World Bank. Created in 1944 at the Bretton Woods Conference, they were originally designed to prevent another Great Depression by stabilizing currency exchange and financing post-war reconstruction.

But by the 1980s, their role had shifted dramatically. As debt crises erupted across the Global South — in Latin America, Sub-Saharan Africa, and Southeast Asia — these institutions became the global enforcers of austerity.

Their tool of choice? Conditional lending — loans offered to countries in financial distress, but only in exchange for:

- Drastic cuts to public spending
- Elimination of food, fuel, and housing subsidies
- Wage freezes and labor deregulation
- Privatization of water, electricity, education, and health systems
- Deregulated capital markets that welcomed

multinational extraction but crushed domestic sovereignty

This "structural adjustment" model — sold as modernization — became the golden rule of debt management for the next 40 years.

But the costs were staggering:

- Hunger in Ghana
- Water riots in Bolivia
- Health system collapse in Zambia
- Mass unemployment in Argentina
- Decades of suppressed wages and stunted infrastructure in Sri Lanka, Pakistan, Tunisia, and beyond

The IMF and World Bank didn't just lend money — they imposed an ideology: scarcity for the poor, deregulation for the rich, and eternal interest for creditors.

Post-scarcity governance demands a clean break.

1. Ending Conditionality That Violates Rights

Conditionality refers to the economic and policy reforms a country must accept to receive IMF or World Bank funding. In the current model, these conditions are determined by technical staff, backed by powerful voting blocs (mainly the U.S. and G7), and enforced without meaningful public input from the countries impacted.

In a rights-based financial system, this must change.

Proposed Reforms:

- Human Rights Screening of All Loan Conditions

- No loan agreement may require cuts to basic services (health, housing, food, education).
- All programs must pass a Wellbeing Impact Assessment (WIA) — with thresholds for nutritional security, shelter access, and infant mortality.
- Participatory Sovereignty in Program Design
  - Borrowing countries must co-design economic programs through public consultations, local civil society panels, and affected community representation.
- UN Oversight Panel on Debt and Rights
  - A new independent body (co-hosted by UNDP and OHCHR) must approve or reject loan conditions based on compatibility with the New Universal Declaration of Economic Rights.
- No Repayment Before Repair
  - Where debt servicing undermines rights fulfillment, countries may delay or restructure payments until benchmarks are met. Creditors share risk.

2. Rebalancing Power: Voting Shares and Representation

Currently, the IMF and World Bank operate on weighted voting systems — where financial contributions determine influence. The United States alone holds veto power at the IMF, and Global South nations remain underrepresented relative to their populations and development challenges.

Proposed Reforms:

- One Nation, One Vote Model for economic rights enforcement decisions
- Permanent Board Seats for African Union, CARICOM, and ASEAN
- Indigenous Economic Councils embedded as formal consultative bodies on land use and development programs
- Civil Society Assemblies with rotating observer status and veto power over anti-rights measures

Without power redistribution, policy reform will remain performative.

3. From Extractive Lending to Reparative Finance

Both the IMF and World Bank have long histories of financing projects that:

- Displace rural and Indigenous communities
- Destroy ecosystems through mega-dams, mining, and fossil fuel infrastructure
- Undermine public goods through privatization and cost-recovery models

Post-scarcity finance requires a new doctrine of harm repair and wealth redirection.
New Lending Mandates:

- Reparative Infrastructure Finance:
    - Prioritize funding for regenerative agriculture, climate-resilient housing, and community-owned energy systems

- Require that all funded projects return social and ecological dividends, not just ROI
- Debt-for-Rights Swaps:
  - Allow countries to cancel portions of sovereign debt by investing directly in public services or ecological restoration
  - Creditor nations get "credit" toward global obligations under the Third Covenant or Trillionaire Stewardship Act
- Public Commons Capital Guarantees:
  - Enable cooperatives, Indigenous communities, and worker-owned enterprises to access World Bank guarantees without private equity backing

4. Transparency, Accountability, and Public Finance Democracy

Post-scarcity international finance must be transparent, traceable, and accountable to the people it affects.

Mechanisms:

- Public Audit of All Development Finance Projects
- Open-source Disclosure of Lending Terms and Contracts
- Right to Consent for Affected Communities — no infrastructure project without free, prior, and informed consent
- Public Scorecards on each institution's alignment with the Third Covenant and Economic Rights metrics

In short: the money must serve life, not leverage.

THE NEW BRETTON WOODS Accord

These reforms can be consolidated into a single binding agreement:

The New Bretton Woods Accord for Economic and Ecological Rights.

Key tenets:

- Debt cannot override dignity
- Lending must advance sufficiency
- Institutions must obey rights
- Power must be democratized

Signed by:

- All Third Covenant nations
- Regional development banks (e.g., AfDB, ADB, CAF)
- Major private creditors seeking legitimacy in a post-rights financial system

RAJ'S RETURN

Back in Colombo, Raj faced a new kind of negotiation. The IMF had not yet signed the Accord — but he had backing from a global coalition. He placed the rights impact audit on the table and said simply:

"We will not trade our hospitals for your spreadsheets.

We'll pay what we owe.

But not at the cost of our people's future."

This time, he didn't blink.

SDRs and Global Wealth Taxes for Universal Human Development

For decades, the global debate around poverty, hunger, and development has revolved around one supposedly inescapable constraint: "There isn't enough money."

This claim is false.

There is more than enough wealth in the world to ensure that every person has access to nutritious food, safe shelter, healthcare, education, clean water, and ecological stability. The issue is not scarcity. It is allocation — and the structures of monetary power that determine who gets to create, control, and deploy financial resources.

To fulfill the promise of the New Universal Declaration of Economic Rights, the world needs a rights-based financial mechanism to:

- Mobilize large-scale public funding
- End dependence on conditional aid
- Redistribute power away from elites and speculative capital
- Fund planetary repair, not planetary degradation

Two tools — one already in use, one urgently needed — offer a path forward:

1. Special Drawing Rights (SDRs) from the International Monetary Fund
2. A Coordinated Global Wealth Tax targeting ultra-high-net-worth individuals and multinational corporations

Together, these instruments form the financial floor of post-scarcity governance.

1. What Are Special Drawing Rights (SDRs)?

SDRs are international reserve assets created by the IMF to supplement countries' official reserves. They aren't a currency per se, but a claim to a basket of currencies (USD, EUR, RMB, JPY, GBP). Countries can exchange SDRs for hard currency during liquidity crises.

In 2021, the IMF issued $650 billion in SDRs — its largest allocation ever — in response to the COVID-19 pandemic.

But here's the problem: distribution is based on IMF quotas, which reflect economic size, not need. That means:

- Wealthy countries received over 60% of the SDRs
- Low-income countries — home to most of the world's poor — received less than 3%

It's as if fire extinguishers were handed out according to building size, not which homes were on fire.

2. Reforming SDRs for Rights-Based Allocation

A post-scarcity approach would repurpose SDRs as global economic rights instruments, not crisis-only liquidity tools.

Key Reforms:

- New SDR Issuances tied to Third Covenant benchmarks:

- Regular allocations every 2–3 years linked to progress on housing, food, health, and climate metrics
- Redistribution Mechanism (Solidarity Swap System):
- High-income countries voluntarily reallocate a percentage of their SDRs to low- and middle-income countries — becoming a binding obligation under the Economic Rights Treaty.
- SDR Trust for Sufficiency Infrastructure:
- Establish a multilateral trust (co-managed by UNDP, OHCHR, and regional banks) that pools reallocated SDRs and disburses them to:
  - Build public hospitals and schools
  - Invest in food sovereignty infrastructure
  - Fund climate adaptation
  - Launch public care programs
- Democratize Governance:
- SDR issuance and distribution decisions to be made by a Global Rights Finance Board, composed of:
  - Global South finance ministers
  - Trillionaire Stewardship Committee observers
  - Labor unions and civil society groups
  - Youth and Indigenous delegates

Bottom line: SDRs must no longer be hoarded as geopolitical reserve assets. They must become fuel for human and ecological flourishing.

. . .

3. The Global Wealth Tax: Ending Economic Immunity for the Ultra-Rich

The second pillar of post-scarcity funding is far more direct: tax the billionaires and trillionaires.

The pandemic made the reality plain:

- Billionaires' wealth increased by $5.2 trillion during a time when over 200 million people were pushed into extreme poverty.
- The world's ten richest individuals hold more wealth than the bottom 3.5 billion combined.
- Trillion-dollar corporations pay single-digit effective tax rates while extracting from public infrastructure, natural resources, and underpaid labor.

This is not economic activity. It is plunder made legal.

4. A Coordinated Global Wealth Tax Framework

From Revenue to Responsibility: Enacting the Global Equity Contribution Protocol (GECP)

The momentum sparked by the OECD's global minimum corporate tax has laid the groundwork for a more ambitious project: coordinated taxation of extreme personal wealth. This isn't merely about funding governments — it's about anchoring a new global social contract based on sufficiency, planetary justice, and participatory prosperity.

The proposed Global Equity Contribution Protocol (GECP) builds on this principle. It envisions a treaty-based framework for taxing ultra-wealthy individuals, harmonized across borders and enforced through integrated financial infrastructure. GECP is not just about fairness; it is the fiscal engine of a post-scarcity governance system.

Key Features of the GECP:

- Wealth Thresholds and Tiered Tax Rates
  - 2% annual tax on net wealth exceeding $100 million
  - 5% annual tax on net wealth exceeding $1 billion
  - 10% annual tax on net wealth exceeding $1 trillion (triggered under *The Trillionaire Stewardship Act*)

These rates are applied progressively — not only collecting revenue but disincentivizing hoarding and reorienting capital toward systems of sufficiency and sustainability.

- Implementation Infrastructure
  - Global Wealth Registries maintained in each signatory country
  - Standardized cross-border tax data-sharing agreements
  - Enforcement mechanisms built into trade, capital flow, and digital banking treaties

This framework not only ensures transparency and accountability but institutionalizes a moral floor beneath capital accumulation, transforming private wealth into public responsibility.

Integrating the Trillionaire Club — From Taxpayer to Steward

The GECP finds its most powerful enforcement mechanism in the Trillionaire Stewardship Act, an international law codifying that:

Any individual whose net wealth exceeds $1 trillion is automatically enrolled in the Trillionaire Club — a global fiduciary body bound by law to steward the planet's basic needs.

This mechanism builds on the proposal detailed The Trillionaire Club Mandate:

- Automatic Membership at $1 Trillion Net Worth
- Members must serve on the Global Human Development and Sufficiency Council, tasked with:
    - Ending global hunger
    - Guaranteeing access to clean water and sanitation
    - Investing in renewable infrastructure and global decarbonization
    - Reversing systems of colonial, ecological, and racial violence
    - Funding a global cooperative care economy
- Trillionaires who fail to comply with GSIF performance mandates face:
    - Asset taxation at up to 100% above $1T
    - Sanctions and asset freezes across treaty-bound jurisdictions
    - Public disclosure of non-cooperation across international media and intergovernmental bodies

This model elevates taxation to a form of constitutional duty — not only financial contribution but active governance participation, proportional to one's economic power.

In this vision, trillionaires become trustees of global equity, not private empires.

Rights-Based Allocation and Global Enforcement

The GECP ensures that the wealth extracted through taxation is not absorbed into existing elite structures, but is earmarked for rights-based global programs through the Global Sufficiency Infrastructure Fund (GSIF):

GSIF Funding Priorities:

1. Universal Basic Services (UBS):
2. • Food, housing, education, and healthcare — enshrined as legal entitlements, not charity.
3. Climate Resilience and Decarbonization:
4. • Mass-scale investment in clean energy, green transit, and land restoration.
5. Reparative Justice:
6. • Funds earmarked for reparations to communities and nations harmed by colonialism, slavery, extractive capitalism, and ecological devastation.
7. Care-Based Economies and Cooperative Development:
8. • Expansion of public child care, elder care, mental health, and cooperative enterprise zones.

The GSIF operates under the Third Covenant, an emerging treaty architecture that updates the Universal Declaration of Human Rights with binding economic and environmental guarantees.

Participation Incentives and Penalties:

- Nations who ratify the GECP gain access to:
  - GSIF project funding
  - Rights-aligned trade agreements
  - Priority access to global innovation networks
- Non-participating jurisdictions face:
  - Financial transaction taxes on all outbound capital
  - Exclusion from rights-aligned trade zones
  - Reputational consequences in ESG (Environmental, Social, Governance) ratings and investment markets

From Global Tax Justice to a Post-Scarcity Future

The Global Equity Contribution Protocol, in concert with The Trillionaire Club framework, is not just a tax proposal — it is a structural transformation. It rewrites the global operating system by treating wealth not as a private entitlement, but as a public trust.

In this new paradigm:

- Wealth above sufficiency is not an escape from responsibility but an entry into stewardship.
- Governance is no longer a domain of states alone — it is shared by the world's most powerful economic actors, under binding law.
- Human dignity and planetary survival are non-negotiable investments, not discretionary expenses.

A coordinated global wealth tax, enforced through GECP and animated by the moral architecture of *The Trillionaire Club*, is how we fund the future — not through scarcity, but through solidarity, sufficiency, and shared sovereignty.

Philosophical Foundation: Wealth as Stewardship, Not Sovereignty

This tax isn't just about raising money. It's about redefining what wealth means.

In a world where unmet need coexists with unimaginable riches, trillionaire status is no longer a private achievement — it is a public jurisdiction.

The Global Wealth Tax operationalizes the idea that:

- Extreme wealth is only legitimate when it serves collective survival
- Those with the most must carry the greatest burden
- Hoarding is not neutral — it is an active form of harm

This is not punishment. It is proportional responsibility in a world of interdependence.

Toward a Fully Funded Future

When combined, SDR reallocation and global wealth taxation form a new social contract:

- Rights are resourced
- Justice is budgeted
- The economy becomes a means to a moral end

And the refrain that "we can't afford it" is finally retired.

Because the truth is:
We can afford dignity.
We just have to choose it.

Role of the Global South and BRICS in Counterbalancing Western Finance Capital

The architecture of global finance has long reflected colonial legacy, creditor supremacy, and dollar dependence.

- The IMF and World Bank are dominated by G7 nations.
- Most capital flows are priced, insured, and cleared through institutions based in New York, London, Frankfurt, and Tokyo.
- Conditionality remains a tool for disciplining the Global South, not empowering it.
- Even development aid often comes with strings: austerity, privatization, deregulation — all dictated from afar.

But history is shifting.

Across Africa, Asia, Latin America, and the Caribbean, countries are refusing to be perpetual clients in a rigged financial order. And at the forefront of this movement stands a coalition increasingly known by one name:

BRICS+

(Brazil, Russia, India, China, South Africa — plus new entrants like Iran, Argentina, Egypt, Ethiopia, and the UAE)

More than a bloc, BRICS+ represents an evolving multipolar force — one that now includes:

- Over 40% of the world's population

- More than 25% of global GDP (PPP-adjusted)
- A shared interest in monetary sovereignty, debt justice, and post-Western development models

This section outlines how the Global South — led in part by BRICS+ — is poised to reshape global finance from the ground up.

1. The Case for Financial Sovereignty

At the heart of Global South frustration is a simple fact: sovereignty without monetary control is a myth.

Most Global South countries:

- Depend on foreign currency reserves to import food and fuel.
- Are vulnerable to U.S. interest rate hikes and dollar volatility.
- Must borrow in hard currencies, then repay with interest often higher than what the Global North pays for its own deficits.
- Face downgrades from ratings agencies for investing in public goods — while fossil fuel expansion earns positive outlooks.

BRICS+ countries are saying no more.
They are building parallel institutions, including:

- The New Development Bank (NDB) – offering no-strings loans for infrastructure, energy, and social investment.
- The Contingent Reserve Arrangement (CRA) – a

$100 billion liquidity pool to reduce reliance on the IMF.
- Proposals for a BRICS settlement currency or blockchain-based clearing mechanism to bypass the SWIFT system and reduce dollar dependency.

2. Aligning BRICS Finance with Economic Rights

For BRICS+ to serve as a post-scarcity force, it must go beyond geopolitics and anchor its financial model in human dignity.

Priorities for a Rights-Aligned BRICS Financial Strategy:

- Adopt the Third Covenant as a shared moral framework for finance and development.
- Integrate economic rights benchmarks into lending and investment criteria (e.g., how many people housed, fed, employed, cared for).
- Fund community-owned renewable energy, public housing, food sovereignty, and universal health systems.
- Create BRICS-based credit rating agencies that reward rights fulfillment and ecological responsibility — not just fiscal contraction.

Outcome: A south-south finance model that replaces austerity with abundance and extraction with repair.

3. Debt Justice, Reparations, and Currency Innovation

A. Debt Audits and Cancellation Mechanisms

- Many Global South debts are odious — incurred by colonial regimes or imposed through coercion.
- BRICS+ can lead a global movement for debt cancellation tied to rights investments (housing, health, food security).
- Launch a South-led International Debt Tribunal to assess the legitimacy of legacy loans and recommend redress.

B. Sovereign Digital Currencies and Payments Infrastructure

- The rise of Central Bank Digital Currencies (CBDCs) offers an opportunity to:
  - Build interoperable systems for direct south-south trade
  - Use smart contracts to trigger rights-based funding disbursements
  - Ensure that digital currency policies respect privacy, transparency, and equitable access

C. Solidarity Reserves and Stabilization Funds

- Establish a Post-Scarcity Resilience Fund, capitalized by BRICS+ member contributions and wealth taxes
- Offer counter-cyclical finance to nations facing shocks from climate, commodity markets, or sanctions

4. Global South Leadership Beyond BRICS

BRICS is just one formation — many others are helping reshape the landscape:

- ALBA (Bolivarian Alliance): Advocating for "life-centric" economics rooted in health, food, and literacy.
- African Union: Advancing African Monetary Institute, continental free trade, and the Pan-African Payment and Settlement System (PAPSS).
- G77 and China: Pushing for fairer trade rules, green technology transfer, and reform of global governance structures.
- CARICOM: Coordinating on food security, climate finance, and reparations for slavery and colonization.

Together, these entities are forging a new economic diplomacy — one grounded in mutual sovereignty, shared provision, and reparative development.

5. Multipolarity Is Not Enough — It Must Be Moral

A multipolar world is not inherently just. BRICS includes authoritarian governments, fossil-fueled economies, and internal inequities.

What matters is the moral framework that guides this multipolarity.

That framework must be:

- Post-extractive: Centering ecology, not empire

- Post-austerity: Centering wellbeing, not fiscal "discipline"
- Post-colonial: Centering reparations and rights, not capital dominance

The Global South isn't just demanding a seat at the table.

It is rebuilding the table — and rewriting the menu.

Toward a Just Financial Future

By coordinating through new institutions, taxing extreme wealth, and issuing rights-based money, the Global South and BRICS+ can:

- Fund sufficiency at scale
- Dismantle neocolonial finance
- Prove that development is not a dollar amount — it is the realization of dignity

And they won't need permission from the old order to do it.

12

GLOBAL RESOURCE STEWARDSHIP AND ECOLOGICAL ECONOMY

Vignette: Tala, a Fisherwoman in the Philippines
Tala paddled her small banca boat out into the bay before sunrise, as her mother and grandmother had done before her. The stars still shimmered above the sea, but the water felt wrong — warmer than usual, with an oily sheen just below the surface.

For generations, her village in Palawan had relied on reef fishing. They took only what was needed, followed lunar tides, honored marine sanctuaries. But in recent years, international trawlers had skirted the laws, stripping the seabed with impunity. The coral was dying. The catch was shrinking. And the community's way of life — their food, income, identity — was dissolving beneath the waves.

One evening, at a community forum led by a local climate organizer, Tala learned about a proposal being advanced at the UN: a new Global Earth Oversight Authority, part of a broader UN Convention on Resource-Based Economic Transition.

Its goal was clear: protect the planet's commons from

profit extraction and place them under global ecological trusteeship.

Tala raised her hand. "Will it stop them from stealing the ocean?"

The organizer smiled. "It can. If enough of us demand it."

Tala looked at her calloused hands and thought of her daughters. Maybe the sea didn't have to die. Maybe the Earth could finally have a lawyer.

Proposal – UN Convention on Resource-Based Economic Transition

For centuries, economic systems have treated the Earth as an infinite warehouse: forests as lumber, rivers as waste disposal, minerals as infinite inputs. Land, water, and biodiversity — once held in sacred trust by Indigenous peoples — have been converted into private assets, traded as commodities, and exploited without regard for limits or reciprocity.

The consequences are everywhere:

- The Amazon, Earth's largest carbon sink, approaching ecological collapse
- Deep-sea mining approved faster than marine ecosystems can be studied
- Groundwater depletion outpacing replenishment in India, Iran, and the U.S. Midwest
- Biodiversity loss so extreme the sixth mass extinction is now underway — caused not by an asteroid, but by economic models

Post-scarcity governance cannot coexist with planetary overshoot.

That's why we need a binding international treaty — a UN Convention on Resource-Based Economic Transition (UN-CRETE) — to transform how we govern the Earth's commons, ensure ecological sustainability, and anchor sufficiency within ecological boundaries.

1. Purpose and Scope of UN-CRETE

The UN Convention on Resource-Based Economic Transition (UN-CRETE) would be the first multilateral treaty to formally declare planetary resources as a shared public trust — governed by ecological science, human rights, and intergenerational equity.

Objectives:

- Shift global economies from price-based allocation to needs-based provisioning
- Legally recognize global commons (air, oceans, climate, biodiversity, freshwater) as non-market domains
- Mandate national and corporate transitions away from extractive resource use
- Create binding legal limits on ecosystem degradation and pollution

This convention becomes the ecological foundation of the Third Covenant — ensuring that economic rights do not come at the expense of planetary rights.

2. Foundational Principles of the Treaty

The Convention rests on five legal and philosophical pillars:

A. *The Earth as a Commons, Not a Commodity*

Natural systems (air, water, forests, climate, soil, biodiversity) belong to no individual or corporation. They are held in trust for all life.

B. *Ecological Sufficiency as a Right and Duty*

All humans have the right to material sufficiency — but not excess. Nations and corporations have a legal obligation to stay within regenerative ecological limits.

C. *Intergenerational Justice*

The rights of future generations are equal in weight to the present — requiring limits on non-renewable resource extraction and carbon emissions.

D. *Free, Prior, and Informed Consent (FPIC)*

Indigenous peoples and frontline communities have sovereign authority over natural systems under their stewardship — and absolute veto power over extractive projects.

E. *Post-Scarcity Transition Timelines*

All signatories must develop and publish Resource Transition Roadmaps by 2030 — detailing how they will phase out extraction, expand commons-based provisioning, and meet sufficiency guarantees within planetary boundaries.

3. Key Provisions and Obligations

   A. *Commons Designation Framework*

- Countries and regions must legally designate the following as non-privatizable commons:
    - Major river systems and aquifers
    - Marine ecosystems and coastal zones
    - Forests with high ecological or cultural value

- Atmosphere and climate system
  - Seed biodiversity, pollinators, and soil fertility zones

B. National Resource Transition Plans (NRTPs)

- All signatory states must submit NRTPs aligned with:
  - Paris Agreement targets
  - IPBES biodiversity metrics
  - Local sufficiency provisioning goals (housing, food, energy, mobility)

These plans are subject to UN-CRETE review and renewal every 3 years.

C. Commons Protection Fund (CPF)

- A multilateral fund financed by:
  - Global wealth taxes
  - Polluter pays penalties
  - Trillionaire Stewardship contributions

The CPF supports:

- Restoration of degraded ecosystems
- Community-led conservation
- Indigenous and traditional ecological knowledge (TEK) systems
- Job guarantees for resource transition workers

D. Corporate Resource Impact Disclosure (CRID)

- All multinational corporations must publish:

- Total natural resource extraction volumes
    - Pollution outputs and ecosystem disruptions
    - Impact on local provisioning capacity (water, food, air)
- Failure to comply triggers international sanctions and removal from public procurement eligibility.

4. Legal Standing and Enforcement
   UN-CRETE would establish:

- The International Tribunal for Ecological Integrity (ITEI)
- Empowered to:
    - Hear cases of commons destruction or treaty violations
    - Issue reparations rulings against states and corporations
    - Enforce moratoria on high-risk extraction projects
- Regional Oversight Councils
- To assess implementation, adjudicate local complaints, and support community enforcement of resource rights.
- Environmental Defenders Protection Protocol
- Ensuring that land defenders, Indigenous leaders, and environmental activists are protected under international law — with redress mechanisms for violence, displacement, or criminalization.

5. Post-Scarcity Through Ecological Stewardship
UN-CRETE is not a constraint on progress — it is the redefinition of progress itself.

In this model:

- Provisioning becomes bioregional and regenerative
- Supply chains shorten, and labor becomes care- and restoration-based
- Sufficiency is measured not in GDP, but in health, beauty, biodiversity, and belonging

This is the world Tala envisioned from her fishing boat — where the ocean is not a battleground for extraction, but a living being under protection.

International Treaty on Commons Protection and Post-Capitalist Trade

The current rules of global trade are written in the language of growth, privatization, and profit maximization.

Whether through the World Trade Organization (WTO), bilateral free trade agreements (FTAs), or corporate-friendly investor-state dispute settlement (ISDS) systems, today's global trade architecture:

- Prioritizes the movement of capital over the rights of people or ecosystems
- Treats public services, seeds, water, and knowledge as commodities
- Locks countries into export-driven models that exhaust soil, water, and labor

- Allows corporations to sue governments for enacting environmental protections
- Undermines local food systems, health sovereignty, and economic self-determination

To transition into a post-scarcity ecological economy, we must rebuild trade from the ground up.

That means replacing the model of global competition with one of commons protection, mutual provisioning, and planetary solidarity.

The International Treaty on Commons Protection and Post-Capitalist Trade (ITCP-PACT) does just that.

1. Purpose of the Treaty

The ITCP-PACT is a binding multilateral agreement designed to:

- Remove global trade incentives that threaten commons and ecological stability
- Protect countries' rights to localize production of essential goods
- Support cooperative, non-extractive modes of cross-border exchange
- Decommodify public goods, knowledge, and natural systems
- Elevate the right to sufficiency above the right to profit

This is trade as relational care — not conquest.

2. Key Principles of Post-Capitalist Trade

The treaty is governed by five foundational principles:

A. Sufficiency First

Trade must support the right to material sufficiency (food, water, housing, health, care), not the accumulation of surplus wealth for the few.

B. Ecological Reciprocity

No trade agreement may override climate targets, biodiversity goals, or local conservation law. Ecocide voids enforceability.

C. Local Sovereignty

Nations and municipalities retain full rights to:

- Protect local industries
- Reject harmful imports
- Prefer cooperatives and worker-owned enterprises in procurement

D. Care and Commons Protections

All public services (water, education, health, transit, energy) are excluded from trade liberalization and investor lawsuits.

E. Democratic Oversight

Trade must be negotiated transparently, with mandatory consultation of labor unions, Indigenous councils, environmental defenders, and frontline communities.

3. Binding Provisions of the Treaty

   A. Commons-Positive Trade Certification

- All traded goods must undergo an ecological and social provisioning impact assessment.

- Goods that violate rights or commons protections are barred from certified trade routes.
- Example bans:
  - Agricultural exports derived from land grabs
  - Water-intensive luxury exports from drought zones
  - Products created through deforestation or forced labor

B. Public Procurement Protections

- Countries can favor local and social enterprises in all public contracts — regardless of WTO or FTA constraints.
- No trade provision may require privatization of public services or commons.

C. Knowledge and Technology Commons

- Patent monopolies on life-saving technologies (vaccines, seeds, energy systems) are abolished under the treaty.
- All nations retain the right to:
  - Share and adapt public innovations
  - Manufacture essential goods without IP restrictions
  - Reject rentier profit claims on Indigenous knowledge

D. Trade and Climate Alignment Clause

- Any trade provision that increases emissions

beyond nationally determined contributions (NDCs) is considered legally void.
- Climate impact assessments are required for:
  - Long-distance exports of non-essential goods
  - Fossil fuel subsidy-linked production
  - Deforestation-risk supply chains

4. Dispute Resolution and Accountability

   A. Abolition of Investor-State Dispute Settlement (ISDS)

- Corporations may no longer sue states in private tribunals for enacting environmental, labor, or public health laws.
- All disputes are heard by the Commons Trade Tribunal, governed by:
  - Public interest lawyers
  - Ecological economists
  - Indigenous legal scholars
  - Cooperative trade federations

   B. Remedy Mechanisms for Harm

- Nations and communities harmed by extractive trade may:
  - Demand reparations
  - Impose restorative trade embargoes
  - Access emergency sufficiency grants from the Commons Protection Fund

   C. Transparent Treaty Review Process

- All signatory trade policies undergo regular Human Rights and Commons Compliance Reviews (HRCCRs), with full civil society participation.

5. Trade in a World Beyond Capital

Post-capitalist trade does not mean isolation or protectionism. It means:

- Trading what communities cannot produce for themselves, not what corporations find most profitable
- Building continental solidarity supply chains, not global race-to-the-bottom outsourcing
- Exchanging knowledge, culture, and care — not just containers and containers of goods

Under this model:

- Cuba and Ghana trade health innovations, not debt
- Bolivia and Sri Lanka exchange agroecology tools, not extractive concessions
- Germany and Kenya co-develop open-source green tech, with no patents attached
- Indigenous seed keepers form transcontinental co-ops, sharing biodiversity under sacred trust

Trade becomes a form of repair — not removal.
An act of dignity — not dominance.

. . .

THE WORLD After the Treaty
Once the ITCP-PACT takes effect:

- WTO rules are superseded by rights law
- Free trade zones become sufficiency zones
- The global economy shifts from conquest to commons care

This is the planetary equivalent of leaving capitalism's house keys behind — and finally moving into a neighborhood where everyone eats, breathes, and thrives together.

IN THE NEXT SECTION, we'll conclude the chapter by proposing a Global Earth Oversight Authority (GEOA) — the coordinating body that brings together planetary science, legal stewardship, and community governance to protect Earth's commons at scale.

Global Earth Oversight Authority (GEOA) — Visionary Governance for Planetary Integrity

The Earth has no legal guardian.

While individual treaties, NGOs, and institutions work to protect species, ecosystems, and climate, there is no single authority charged with defending the Earth as a living system — with standing in law, enforcement tools, and a mandate to represent present and future generations.

In today's geopolitical system, no institution exists that can:

- Prevent ecological collapse before it happens

- Hold states and corporations accountable for planetary harm
- Harmonize biodiversity, climate, and resource treaties into a coherent governance structure
- Represent the rights of ecosystems, Indigenous knowledge holders, and unborn generations

That is the role of the Global Earth Oversight Authority (GEOA) — the visionary body proposed to coordinate and enforce the commitments of the UN Convention on Resource-Based Economic Transition and the International Treaty on Commons Protection and Post-Capitalist Trade.

1. Why GEOA Is Needed

Consider the fragmented reality:

- Biodiversity is governed by the Convention on Biological Diversity (CBD)
- Climate is addressed by the UNFCCC and the IPCC, which has no enforcement power
- Water access and forest protection are scattered across dozens of overlapping frameworks
- Global trade regimes often undermine ecological protections

Meanwhile:

- No single body holds legal power to protect global commons
- Earth system thresholds (e.g. safe CO_2 levels, freshwater use, nitrogen cycles) are being crossed without consequence

- Ecocide is not yet an enforceable international crime

In short: the Earth has symptoms of governance — but not a governing body.
GEOA is designed to fill that gap.

2. Structure and Mandate of the GEOA

The Global Earth Oversight Authority (GEOA) is a proposed independent agency within the United Nations, established by treaty and guided by ecological law, Earth system science, and human rights.

Core Mandate:

- Enforce ecological boundaries and planetary thresholds
- Hold violators (states or corporations) accountable for ecocide and commons harm
- Certify global sufficiency within ecological limits
- Coordinate implementation of all treaties tied to the Third Covenant and post-scarcity governance

3. Key Powers and Functions

A. Planetary Threshold Monitoring

- Track nine core Earth system boundaries (based on Rockström et al.'s planetary boundaries model), including:
  - Atmospheric CO_2 concentration
  - Ocean acidification

- Biosphere integrity
- Freshwater use
- Chemical pollution
- Nitrogen/phosphorus cycling
- Land system change
* Publish real-time dashboards and country-specific reports showing progress or overshoot

B. Commons Certification System

* Certify regions, cities, and countries as Commons Guardians, based on:
  - Protection of local ecosystems
  - Compliance with rights-based provisioning
  - Elimination of ecologically harmful trade practices
* Issue Commons Impact Ratings for corporations and financial institutions, influencing investment flows

C. Enforcement Tools

* Impose ecological reparations, sanctions, and trade restrictions on:
  - Countries that violate planetary boundaries
  - Corporations that destroy protected commons
  - States that criminalize environmental defenders
* Coordinate with the International Tribunal for Ecological Integrity (ITEI) to enforce rulings

D. Restorative Justice and Planetary Repair

- Operate a Global Restoration Fund using:
  - Trillionaire Stewardship Act contributions
  - International Wealth Taxes
  - Commons Trade revenue
- Fund:
  - Reforestation and Indigenous land return
  - Coastal and marine habitat restoration
  - Soil regeneration and seed biodiversity programs
  - Public works jobs focused on ecological repair

4. Representation and Governance
GEOA is governed by a Tri-Chamber Assembly:

1. Ecological Science Council

- Composed of climate scientists, Indigenous ecologists, Earth system modelers, biodiversity experts
- Establishes planetary thresholds, evaluates data, and issues binding ecological recommendations

2. Peoples' Assembly for Planetary Justice

- Elected from every continent, with guaranteed representation for:
  - Indigenous nations
  - Women and youth
  - Small island states
  - Environmental defenders
  - Rural and frontline communities

- Holds veto power over extractive exceptions and major infrastructure projects

3. Global Commons Judiciary Panel

- A judicial branch interpreting ecological law and rights of nature claims
- Resolves conflicts between states, corporations, and communities

5. The Legal Recognition of Earth as a Living Being

A foundational act of the GEOA is to declare legal personhood and rights of existence for:

- The Amazon Rainforest
- The Great Barrier Reef
- The Congo Basin
- Major freshwater systems (Amazon, Nile, Mekong, Mississippi, Danube)
- Ocean zones and atmospheric layers

This builds upon precedents already set by:

- Ecuador's constitutional recognition of nature's rights
- New Zealand's recognition of the Whanganui River as a legal person
- Colombia's court rulings protecting the Amazon and Atrato rivers

GEOA becomes the guardian of the planet's voice in law.

. . .

6. The World with GEOA
   Imagine:

   - A major fossil fuel company blocked from new exploration by a GEOA ruling
   - A desertified region restored through commons investment and carbon drawdown jobs
   - Small nations with few emissions but high vulnerability given veto power over planetary decisions
   - Trade agreements rewritten to pass planetary integrity review before approval

This is ecological democracy at scale — not managed from boardrooms, but co-governed by the Earth's inhabitants and ecosystems themselves.

A PLANETARY SYSTEM for a Planetary Crisis
GEOA is not an environmental agency.
It is:

- A planetary insurance policy
- A justice mechanism for the biosphere
- A democratic redesign of global ecological governance

Because if we can have global systems to manage banks, borders, and bombs —
Surely we can have one to protect life itself.

13

EDUCATION AS ECONOMIC LIBERATION

Vignette: Ayana, a Literacy Volunteer in Detroit

Ayana flipped through a dog-eared copy of *The Autobiography of Malcolm X* as her students filed into the community center. She taught literacy three nights a week — mostly to adults who had fallen through the cracks of a system that had never really seen them.

One of her students, Marcus, had spent 12 years in prison. Another, Gloria, had dropped out of high school to care for her siblings. Ayana didn't just teach them how to read — she helped them decode the system that had failed them.

Tonight's lesson was different. On the whiteboard, Ayana had written:

"What is the purpose of an economy?"

They read a passage from a new report issued by the Post-Scarcity Transition Council. It proposed a future where everyone had guaranteed housing, food, health care, and education — not as privileges, but rights.

Gloria raised her hand.

"So why didn't they teach us this in school?"

Ayana didn't answer right away.

"Because an educated population might stop accepting scarcity as normal."

Marcus nodded. "Then let's get dangerous."

National Curriculum for Economic Literacy, Civic Participation, and Critical Systems Thinking

Education is not neutral.

What a society teaches — and chooses not to teach — reflects what it values, fears, and intends to reproduce.

For the past century, most national education systems have trained citizens to:

- Obey authority
- Accept economic precarity as natural
- Conflate success with individual competition
- Trust corporate solutions to public problems
- Learn just enough to participate in markets, but not enough to question them

This was by design.

As global economic inequality deepens, climate crisis accelerates, and democracy teeters, it's clear that this educational model is not preparing people to survive — let alone transform — the 21st century.

A post-scarcity future demands a radically new approach to education:

- One that teaches how economies function — and for whom
- One that demystifies power, policy, and public budgeting

- One that trains people to recognize interdependence, organize collectively, and design new systems

In short, it demands education as economic liberation.

1. Economic Literacy: Understanding the Rules of the Game

Most people don't learn how the economy works — they learn how to work within it. This isn't education. It's conditioning.

In a post-scarcity curriculum, students of all ages learn to understand:

- Where money comes from (monetary policy, banking, government spending)
- How budgets reflect values, not just math
- What taxation does (redistribution, behavior shaping, civic prioritization)
- Who writes the rules (corporations, governments, international bodies — and how to influence them)
- The false narratives of trickle-down economics, "balanced budgets," and bootstrapping myths
- The structure and purpose of public goods, commons, and social guarantees

By high school, every student should be able to answer:

- Who owns your utilities?
- How is your local budget set?
- Who profits from your housing situation?

- How do financial markets impact your cost of living?

Informed citizens are unruly citizens — and that's the point.

2. Civic Participation: Practicing Power from the Classroom Up

Democracy must be practiced to be real. Voting every few years is not enough — especially when power is concentrated in unelected boards, corporate lobbies, and international trade tribunals.

Civic education, in a post-scarcity context, becomes:

- Embodied — students co-govern their classrooms, design budgets, and resolve conflicts through participatory processes
- Community-integrated — youth collaborate with city councils, mutual aid groups, and workers' co-ops
- Experiential — mock legislatures, simulation of budget tradeoffs, and real-world policy design

Every student should graduate having:

- Participated in at least one participatory budgeting process
- Met with a local or state legislator about an issue they researched
- Practiced public testimony, negotiation, and coalition-building

- Explored their own neighborhood's history of resistance and resilience

This isn't "civics" as flag-waving. It's civic capability as a right and responsibility.

Because if you can't access the levers of power, you don't live in a democracy — you live in an illusion of one.

3. Critical Systems Thinking: Teaching Interdependence and Design

The world is not made up of isolated problems. It's composed of systems — interconnected, often invisible, complex networks of cause and effect.

Post-scarcity education equips students to see:

- The feedback loops between climate, poverty, health, and housing
- How individual outcomes emerge from structural design
- The role of values and paradigms in shaping institutions

This isn't abstract.
It means teaching:

- How zoning codes shape racial segregation
- How logistics infrastructure links labor exploitation and carbon emissions
- How gendered assumptions in care work policy affect GDP and family health

It means interdisciplinary projects where students map:

- The life cycle of a loaf of bread
- The carbon cost of digital storage
- The global supply chain behind a cell phone
- The community ecosystem around a neighborhood library

And most importantly, it means teaching design:

- How to prototype policies
- How to co-create solutions with users
- How to run deliberative assemblies and citizen juries
- How to iterate on governance systems, not just accept them

From Consumers to Creators of the Future

The goal of post-scarcity education is not job readiness — it's justice readiness.

We need citizens who can:

- See through scarcity myths
- Organize for rights, not charity
- Envision alternatives and build prototypes
- Hold power to account, even when it wears a suit or brand name
- Practice care, cooperation, and imagination at every level of society

Economic literacy is self-defense.
Civic power is public safety.
Systems thinking is how we turn knowledge into

liberation.

In the next section, we'll explore how decentralized media cooperatives and narrative sovereignty can amplify this education — ensuring that the tools of storytelling, information, and identity are reclaimed from platforms of manipulation and turned toward movements of collective truth.

Decentralized Media Cooperatives and Narrative Sovereignty

You can't build a new world with an old story.

Every economic system is powered not just by material resources, but by narratives — the stories we tell about what's possible, what's desirable, what's inevitable, and what's "just the way things are."

Under neoliberal capitalism, mass media has functioned as:

- A myth factory, normalizing wealth inequality, consumerism, and meritocracy
- A gatekeeper, marginalizing dissenting voices and alternative paradigms
- A megaphone for the powerful, amplifying corporate interests while silencing grassroots truth
- A mirror that distorts, projecting insecurity, scarcity, and hyperindividualism

If education is how we learn to think, then media is how we learn to feel — about ourselves, each other, and the future.

That's why post-scarcity governance requires not just

new schools and curriculums, but new cultural infrastructures: spaces where people can see themselves, shape the narrative, and reclaim their story.

1. The Need for Narrative Sovereignty
Narrative sovereignty is the right of communities to:

- Create and control their own representations
- Tell their own histories and future visions
- Communicate without gatekeepers or exploitative platforms
- Shape the dominant metaphors and frames that structure social meaning

This isn't just about media access — it's about media ownership, cultural dignity, and epistemic justice.

Because for generations:

- Indigenous voices were erased from environmental debates
- Black resistance was criminalized in the press
- Poor people's stories were told without them
- Women were shown but not heard
- Labor was aestheticized, but not politicized

And all the while, corporate media platforms became global empires — commodifying attention, harvesting emotion, and monetizing misinformation.

2. Decentralized Media Cooperatives: A New Infrastructure for Public Truth

Post-scarcity societies build decentralized, cooperative, and community-anchored media ecosystems.

These are not side projects — they are democratic necessities.

Features of Media Cooperatives:

- Owned and governed by workers and/or communities
- Non-profit or surplus-reinvested into education, investigative journalism, and public tech
- Multi-format: radio, print, podcasts, film, open-access research, community TikToks
- Funded through commons-based models: public grants, platform dividends, solidarity subscriptions

Key Functions:

- Local news production rooted in community priorities
- Political education programming for all ages
- Crisis response networks to counter misinformation during climate, health, or political shocks
- Cultural storytelling that heals trauma, celebrates resistance, and lifts futures not yet imagined

3. Platform Cooperativism: Reclaiming Digital Spaces

Media cooperatives are physical and cultural, but also digital.

Platform cooperativism is the idea that the digital platforms we rely on — for news, communication, learning, and organizing — should be collectively owned and democratically governed.

Imagine:

- A Wikipedia-style news ecosystem where contributors are paid, fact-checked, and context-aware
- A video platform like YouTube, but free from ad tracking, algorithmic bias, and disinformation incentives
- A social media space where users elect moderators, set policies, and share in the value they create
- Decentralized mesh networks that allow communities to stay online during disasters or shutdowns

These aren't just tech fantasies. Projects like Open Collective, DisCO, Civic Signals, Ampled, and Hypha are already prototyping this future.

In a post-scarcity economy, they become public infrastructure — not private ventures.

4. Training a Generation of Media Justice Builders

To power these ecosystems, post-scarcity education must train:

- Investigative journalists grounded in justice
- Media-makers fluent in local languages and histories

- Technologists who build for transparency, not surveillance
- Artists and archivists who preserve truth and amplify resistance
- Educators who treat media literacy as civic empowerment

And just as every citizen must be economically literate, they must also be narratively literate:

- Able to spot propaganda
- Understand how stories shape public policy
- Recognize frame bias, source manipulation, and emotional priming
- Tell their own story in the language of collective power

5. Countering Narrative Scarcity

In the old paradigm, there was a story for everything — except justice.

- A child in poverty? "Bad choices."
- A country in debt? "They lived beyond their means."
- A climate refugee? "Illegal migrant."
- A billionaire? "Self-made genius."
- A hungry nation? "Corrupt leadership."

These aren't explanations. They're weapons disguised as wisdom.

Post-scarcity media dismantles these frames. It builds new narratives, such as:

- "You are not a burden — you are a birthright."
- "Debt is not a sin — it's a system."
- "Freedom is not found in markets — it's built in community."

This is how liberation becomes believable — and belief becomes action.

From Propaganda to Possibility

When the people control the story, the system can't hold.

Because in the story of post-scarcity, there are no "deserving poor" — only undeserved poverty.

No "developed" vs "developing" — only a world still learning to care.

No "job creators" — only people building the future, together.

A free society needs free press — not just from censorship, but from capital.

And a post-scarcity world needs storytellers who remember:

The most powerful truth is the one we build with our lives.

Movement Infrastructure and Civic Governance

A liberated society cannot be sustained by inspiration alone.

Marches, uprisings, and viral campaigns matter — but without infrastructure, movements stall. Ideas fade. Policies backslide. Justice retreats. Transformation becomes memory instead of future.

If post-scarcity is to be more than a manifesto — if it is to be a system — we must build movements like we build cities: with blueprints, materials, networks, utilities, and maintenance plans.

This chapter lays out the civic backbone of that transformation: the strategic alliances, governance models, and digital platforms that turn passion into power, and vision into permanence.

1. Strategic Alliance of Climate, Justice, Labor, and Tech Movements

Post-scarcity transformation does not belong to one cause. It requires a coalition of coalitions — united not by identical tactics, but by shared values and structural demands.

Core Movement Convergence:

- Climate Justice: Advocating for decarbonization, land back, and ecological repair
- Economic Justice: Demanding food, housing, care, and debt cancellation as rights
- Labor and Workers' Rights: Advancing union democracy, co-determination, and job guarantees
- Tech Justice: Reclaiming digital infrastructure for public use and ethical design
- Abolition and Racial Justice: Ending carceral systems and reinvesting in life-affirming institutions
- Feminist and Care Movements: Centering

unpaid labor, reproductive autonomy, and time sovereignty

These movements already exist — often fragmented, sometimes in competition. Post-scarcity governance braids them together, recognizing that:

- Housing policy is climate policy
- Labor justice is care justice
- Food sovereignty is anti-racist, anti-colonial economic design
- Data governance is civic governance

Slogan alignment is not enough. Shared infrastructure is essential.

2. The Post-Scarcity Congress: A Shadow Parliament of the People

Proposed as part of the Trillionaire Stewardship Act, the Post-Scarcity Congress is a non-state, semi-formal global civic body that:

- Gathers representatives from frontline movements, cooperatives, unions, and civil society networks
- Drafts people's budgets, rights-based policies, and participatory alternatives to extractive governance
- Tracks compliance with economic rights, post-scarcity goals, and Third Covenant implementation

Structure:

- Elected via networked constituencies (e.g., climate hubs, regional assemblies, food sovereignty alliances)
- Decisions made through deliberative democracy tools and consensus processes
- Publishes the annual State of Sufficiency Report, benchmarking global progress on rights fulfillment

Function:
Not to replace existing legislatures, but to pressure, prototype, and legitimize alternatives — becoming the moral and strategic conscience of planetary democracy.

3. Tools: Participatory AI, Blockchain for Public Goods, Commons-Based Governance Models

No movement infrastructure is complete without digital tools designed for democracy, not surveillance.

A. Participatory Artificial Intelligence

- AI models trained on justice-oriented data, co-governed by civic councils
- Use cases:
    - Policy simulation tools (e.g., "What happens if we cut rent by 50%?")
    - Resource matching (connecting surplus food to hunger zones in real time)
    - Dynamic budget forecasting (projecting long-term impacts of sufficiency policies)

B. Commons-Based Blockchain Systems

- Not for speculation — for transparency, trust, and traceability
- Use cases:
    - Public benefit registries (who receives what, with what outcome)
    - Commons ownership verification (e.g., land trusts, co-ops)
    - Timebank and mutual credit networks (care labor tracking, skill sharing)

C. Open-Governance Platforms

- Local, national, and transnational portals where citizens:
    - Submit policy proposals
    - Vote on spending priorities
    - Deliberate with real-time interpretation and accessibility tools
    - Receive feedback on how their input shapes law

Examples already in use:

- Decidim in Barcelona
- vTaiwan in Taiwan
- Loomio in global co-op networks

These tools aren't substitutes for organizing — they're amplifiers of agency.

. . .

4. Movement Institutions: Anchoring Power for the Long Term

Flash activism doesn't build new worlds. Institution-building does.

Essential Movement Institutions:

- People's Policy Schools – teaching systems thinking, campaign design, and power mapping
- Sufficiency Research Hubs – conducting independent evaluations of post-scarcity progress
- Movement Libraries and Archives – preserving the knowledge of resistance and success
- Public Interest Legal Clinics – supporting the implementation and defense of economic rights
- Co-op Incubators and Solidarity Funds – turning protest into enterprise with values intact

These institutions must be:

- Federated, not centralized
- Community-led, not expert-dominated
- Designed to last 100 years, not one election cycle

5. Cultural Rituals and Civic Mythologies

Every durable system is sustained not just by policy, but by ritual and story:

- Harvest festivals linked to food sovereignty
- Days of remembrance for housing liberation struggles

- Rites of passage into cooperative membership or community stewardship

In post-scarcity societies, civic identity becomes collective and creative — not passive or consumerist.
Imagine:

- "Day of Enough": Annual holiday where communities reflect on sufficiency, share resources, and celebrate planetary boundaries
- "Budget Assemblies": Neighborhoods gather to allocate public funds together, hosted as cultural events with food, music, and child care
- "Commons Citizenship Ceremonies": Honoring new members of co-ops, care networks, or land trusts with solemnity and joy

These are the emotional glue of transformation.

A Blueprint for Power That Lasts

We cannot educate our way out of oppression if we don't organize.

We cannot organize our way to liberation if we don't govern.

We cannot govern if we do not build.

Movements that win do not simply protest — they provision.

They don't just demand rights — they institute justice.

This is the infrastructure we must build — to make freedom not just felt, but formalized.

14
A MANDATE FOR MORAL IMAGINATION

"*We are not waiting for permission. We are claiming our role in the remaking of the world.*"

THE SYSTEMS that brought us here — to a world of engineered scarcity, ecological collapse, billionaires in bunkers, and children without dinner — were designed.

They were made by people.

Which means they can be unmade — and remade.

This book has laid out the blueprint:

- An economic model grounded in rights, not revenue
- A legal framework for sufficiency and stewardship
- Institutional pathways at the local, national, and international levels
- Funding strategies drawn from existing tools and radical honesty

- Cultural and educational scaffolding to ensure longevity
- A redefinition of wealth, power, and justice — from extraction to care

I have shown that post-scarcity is not utopian — it is overdue.

I have proven that cost is no excuse — because inequality is already unaffordable.

I have demonstrated that the capacity exists — in budgets, in communities, in technologies, and most importantly, in people who are done pretending that dystopia is our only option.

A Decade-by-Decade Roadmap (2025–2100)

To make post-scarcity more than policy — to make it culture, governance, and default reality — we propose the following global progression:

2025–2035: The Foundation

- Pass sufficiency-centered legislation at municipal, regional, and federal levels (see Chapters 14–16)
- Launch Universal Basic Services pilots and post-scarcity budgeting practices
- Ratify the Third Covenant on Economic and Ecological Rights
- Reorient Bretton Woods institutions toward rights-based lending
- Establish Commons Trusts, Global Earth Oversight Authority (GEOA), and regional abundance alliances

- Implement wealth taxes and the Trillionaire Stewardship clause

2035–2050: The Transition

- Phase out scarcity-based budgeting, welfare conditionality, and extractive GDP policy
- Global rollout of post-capitalist trade frameworks (see ITCP-PACT)
- Formal end of ecocide impunity via international court enforcement
- All education systems include civic design, narrative sovereignty, and economic literacy
- Climate-safe job guarantees standard across all nations
- Ecological footprint per capita stabilized within planetary boundaries

2050–2100: The Maturation

- Full global sufficiency: Zero hunger, homelessness, or uninsurance
- Rights of nature enshrined in constitutional and international law
- Commons provisioning becomes primary mode of local economic design
- Civil society-led governance coalitions outpace corporate multinationals in scale and trust
- Intergenerational councils embedded in lawmaking
- Earth systems show net repair — not net damage

Bridging Realism with Vision

Some will say this is naive.

That people are selfish. That politics is too broken. That markets are inevitable. That nothing changes.

But history tells a different story.

- Slavery was law — until people refused
- Women were property — until they weren't
- Monarchies were destiny — until the people claimed voice
- Fossil fuel dominance seemed permanent — until the Earth began to burn

Every impossibility is just a story that hasn't yet met enough courage.

Moral imagination is not fantasy. It is the discipline of seeing the world not only as it is, but as it could be — and acting from that place before the proof exists.

15

FROM DIAGNOSIS TO COLLECTIVE DESIGN

This book has diagnosed:

- The violent logic of scarcity
- The failure of reform within toxic systems
- The weapons of finance, law, narrative, and governance that hold the world hostage

But it has also designed:

- A rights-based world, funded and enforceable
- Local and global frameworks to build it
- Cultural rituals to sustain it
- Legal tools to defend it
- A moral economy where freedom is not a luxury

Now it's your turn.
To build.
To organize.
To govern.

To rest.
To dream again.
To practice tomorrow — now.

From Scarcity to Stewardship

We end not with an answer, but with a mandate:

If you can house the unhoused, do it.

If you can feed the hungry, do it.

If you can write the law, paint the mural, start the school, convene the circle, repair the harm, pass the charter — do it.

If you can do any of this, you are already part of the future.

And if you doubt that such a world is possible, remember:

The only thing scarcer than abundance in the old system... was the courage to imagine something better.

Now you have the map.

The time is yours.

ABOUT THE AUTHOR

JD Rossetti is a seasoned public affairs professional, which is a fancy way of saying he's spent over a decade navigating the world of government relations, legislative affairs, public administration, and policy analysis—without losing his sense of humor (or his hair... mostly). With a knack for advocacy, strategic planning, and community engagement, JD has dedicated his career to shaping public policy and making a real difference.

A former Washington State Representative, JD tackled big issues like education, infrastructure, economic development, and public health—because someone had to. He successfully secured funding for education, mental health initiatives, and broadband expansion, ensuring that students could learn, communities could thrive, and people could finally stream their favorite shows without buffering. As a School Board Director, he championed student success, technology integration, and budget oversight, proving that yes, numbers can be fun (sometimes).

JD holds a Master of Public Administration (MPA) from The Evergreen State College and a Bachelor of Arts in Public Affairs from Washington State University. Passionate about public service, policy innovation, and effective governance, JD continues to work toward policies that strengthen and support communities—one well-crafted policy (and dad joke) at a time.

APPENDICES

First they ignore you.
Then they laugh at you.
Then they fight you.
Then you win.

DRAFTING TOMORROW – SAMPLE UNITED NATIONS RESOLUTION

Title: "Declaration for the Advancement of Economic and Ecological Abundance for All Peoples"
Resolution Number: (To be assigned upon General Assembly submission)

Submitted by: [Sponsoring Member States:]

Agenda Item: Economic and Social Development; Climate Justice and Sustainable Development Goals (SDGs)

Preamble
The General Assembly,
Recalling the Universal Declaration of Human Rights (1948),
Recognizing the International Covenant on Economic, Social, and Cultural Rights (1966),
Acknowledging the Paris Agreement on Climate Change (2015), the SDG Agenda (2030), and the Convention on Biological Diversity (1992),
Noting with grave concern the persistent global failure

to eradicate hunger, homelessness, preventable disease, and ecological destruction in an era of unprecedented global wealth and technological advancement,

Affirming that economic deprivation and ecological collapse are preventable and constitute violations of human dignity and justice,

Understanding that the current dominant economic paradigm, centered on scarcity, GDP growth, and extractivism, is incompatible with planetary limits and human flourishing,

Believing that a new paradigm of economic and ecological abundance, grounded in rights-based sufficiency and global stewardship, is both possible and necessary,

Recognizing the leadership of civil society, Indigenous peoples, youth, women, and grassroots movements in advancing transformative alternatives,

Declarations

The General Assembly hereby proclaims the following:

Article 1: The Right to Economic and Ecological Abundance

All peoples have the right to live in a world where:

- Material sufficiency — including food, housing, healthcare, education, energy, and time — is guaranteed
- Ecological systems are protected and restored for current and future generations
- Public goods are prioritized over private wealth accumulation
- Dignity is not conditional on employment, citizenship, or economic productivity

Article 2: Post-Scarcity as a Global Development Goal

Member States shall:

- Transition from GDP-centric policy to well-being-centered metrics
- Develop national strategies to ensure universal basic services
- Align fiscal and monetary systems with the provisioning of human and ecological needs
- Commit to ecological ceilings and social foundations as defined by the Doughnut Economics and Planetary Boundaries frameworks

Article 3: Global Redistribution and Sovereignty
Member States recognize that:

- Extreme wealth accumulation is incompatible with sustainable sufficiency
- Financial and natural resources must be redistributed through progressive taxation, reparations, and public ownership mechanisms
- Global South nations have the right to self-determined development free from illegitimate debt and structural adjustment

Article 4: Commons Protection and Stewardship
Natural resources essential to life — including water, forests, seeds, biodiversity, and the atmosphere — shall be:

- Governed as global and local commons
- Protected from privatization, pollution, or commodification

- Stewarded through participatory governance by communities and Indigenous peoples

Article 5: Governance and Legal Transformation
The General Assembly supports:

- The drafting of a Third International Covenant on Economic and Ecological Rights
- The recognition of Ecocide as a crime under international law
- The establishment of a Global Earth Oversight Authority (GEOA)
- The democratization of international financial institutions including the IMF and World Bank
- The creation of a Global Sufficiency Infrastructure Fund, financed by global wealth taxes and solidarity contributions

Article 6: Cultural, Educational, and Technological Transformation
Member States shall:

- Incorporate economic literacy and ecological consciousness into all levels of education
- Support the development of publicly owned media and narrative sovereignty platforms
- Fund technological innovation that serves the common good, not speculative capital
- Promote arts and culture that envision and advance the world of sufficiency and repair

Implementation and Follow-Up
　A. Voluntary National Abundance Reports

Member States are invited to submit National Abundance Reports to the Secretary-General every two years, outlining progress on:

- Universal access to basic services
- Transition to ecological economies
- Community commons governance
- Reduction of wealth inequality and material precarity

B. Establishment of an Abundance Transition Task Force
The UN shall establish an interagency Task Force on Economic and Ecological Abundance, with participation from:

- UNDP, OHCHR, UNEP, FAO, ILO, UNESCO
- Civil society and Indigenous networks
- BRICS+, G77, and Global North allies

The Task Force will develop:

- Legal guidance for the Third Covenant
- Transition frameworks for economic systems
- Monitoring tools for sufficiency implementation

Final Declaration
"We, the peoples of the United Nations, declare that poverty, hunger, and ecological destruction are not natural — they are the results of policy, ideology, and political will.

We therefore commit to building a world where abundance is no longer the privilege of a few, but the shared inheritance of all."

DRAFTING TOMORROW – SAMPLE U.S. LEGISLATION

Full Annotated Draft of the Post-Scarcity Economic Transformation Act

"To guarantee all persons in the United States the right to material sufficiency, establish the legal foundation for a post-scarcity economy, and reorient federal governance toward the universal provisioning of core human needs within ecological limits."

Section 1: Short Title

This Act may be cited as the Post-Scarcity Economic Transformation Act of 2025 (hereinafter "the Act").

Section 2: Congressional Findings and Purpose
Findings:

1. Every person has the inherent right to sufficient food, housing, healthcare, education, energy, mobility, and time to live with dignity.
2. Current economic models have failed to secure these rights for tens of millions of U.S. residents.

3. Structural scarcity is a policy choice, not a natural condition.
4. Ecological overshoot and wealth inequality threaten national and global stability.
5. The federal government has the fiscal capacity and constitutional authority to fulfill these rights through legislative and executive action.

Purpose:
To establish a national legal framework for:

- Universal Basic Services
- Post-scarcity economic metrics
- Institutional transformation of federal agencies
- Community-driven provisioning models
- Constitutional alignment with sufficiency guarantees

Section 3: Definitions

- Sufficiency: The condition of having one's essential needs met without deprivation or precarity.
- Universal Basic Services (UBS): A federally guaranteed bundle of rights including housing, food, health care, education, mobility, energy, and digital access.
- Post-Scarcity Economy: An economic system organized around meeting human needs and maintaining ecological integrity rather than maximizing profit or GDP.
- Ecological Floor: The minimum biospheric health needed to support life systems.

- Social Ceiling: The point at which material excess harms others or the planet.

Section 4: Right to Sufficiency
A new Federal Right to Sufficiency is hereby established. Every U.S. resident shall have:

- Secure housing without threat of eviction or homelessness
- Nutritious food accessible without stigma or scarcity
- Healthcare free at the point of use
- Access to quality education, mobility, and communication
- Legal redress in cases where these rights are denied due to policy, funding gaps, or exclusion

Section 5: National Sufficiency Dashboard
The Bureau of Economic Analysis (BEA), in collaboration with the Departments of Health and Human Services, Housing and Urban Development, Energy, Agriculture, and Education, shall publish a National Sufficiency Dashboard quarterly, including metrics such as:

- % of population with secure housing
- Number of medically uninsured individuals
- Food insecurity rates
- Access to broadband internet
- Educational access and outcomes by geography and race
- Regional ecological depletion thresholds

All federal budget proposals must include a Sufficiency Impact Assessment.

Section 6: Universal Basic Services Framework

Establish the Office of Universal Basic Services (OUBS) within the Executive Office of the President to:

- Coordinate interagency provisioning of UBS
- Monitor compliance with rights guarantees
- Issue guidance to states for implementation with federal block grants
- Establish minimum national standards for UBS delivery

Mandates include:

- Construction of public housing and retrofits (HUD)
- Expansion of public clinics and mental health services (HHS)
- Public food cooperatives and urban agriculture grants (USDA)
- Public broadband and digital equity (FCC + Department of Commerce)

Section 7: Sufficiency Jobs Guarantee

The Department of Labor shall develop a Sufficiency Sector Jobs Program:

- Federally funded employment in:
    - Housing construction
    - Food systems and regenerative agriculture
    - Climate resilience infrastructure

- Public caregiving, eldercare, and child development
- Education, literacy, and arts

All jobs are paid living wages with full benefits, union rights, and career advancement pathways.

Section 8: Institutional Reorientation
Amend agency mandates to reflect sufficiency over scarcity:

Federal Reserve

- Expand dual mandate to include:
  - Full employment with sufficiency outcomes
  - Equitable access to credit for public purpose
  - Regulation of speculative lending that threatens UBS

Department of Commerce

- Replace GDP as primary policy indicator with WELLBYs (Wellbeing-Adjusted Life Years) and Social Return on Investment (SROI)

Department of Defense

- Redirect a portion of budget toward climate adaptation, logistics for food and water provisioning, and disaster response coordination

Section 9: Funding and Fiscal Tools
This Act authorizes:

- Use of sovereign monetary financing to fund UBS (via coordination with the Fed under Treasury issuance)
- Wealth tax implementation above $100M to support UBS Infrastructure Fund
- Redirection of fossil fuel subsidies toward housing, food, and care provisioning
- Creation of Public Goods Bonds accessible to credit unions and community banks

Section 10: Enforcement and Justiciability

- Residents may bring suit in federal court if:
  - Denied UBS due to state noncompliance
  - Harmed by discriminatory policies in access to sufficiency rights
  - Agencies fail to meet minimum provisioning benchmarks
- Establish Office of Sufficiency Rights under DOJ to coordinate legal responses, settlements, and class actions.

Section 11: State Partnership Incentives

States may:

- Join National Sufficiency Compact
- Receive tiered implementation grants
- Design community-driven provisioning models, including:
  - Mutual aid partnerships
  - Tribal governance integration
  - Cooperative municipal UBS agencies

Section 12: Emergency Sufficiency Response Authority
In declared economic or climate emergencies:

- Federal government may:
    - Seize and repurpose vacant properties for shelter
    - Mandate production of food and energy goods
    - Distribute universal aid through USPS, FEMA, and local governance hubs
    - Suspend debt and utility payments for low-income households

Section 13: Public Engagement and Education
The Act mandates:

- National campaign for economic literacy, sufficiency rights, and participatory governance
- Curriculum changes in public schools to include:
    - Systems thinking
    - Budget transparency
    - Commons and cooperative economics

Section 14: Effective Dates

- All reporting and dashboard mechanisms shall begin within 12 months
- Sufficiency Rights become enforceable 24 months from enactment
- UBS Office operational within 18 months
- Full sufficiency coverage to be achieved by 2035, with annual review benchmarks

Final Note:

This Act shall be known not only as law — but as a living promise.

That in the richest nation on Earth, no one will go without, and no future will be held hostage by old myths of what we can afford.

DRAFTING TOMORROW – SAMPLE CHARTER FOR CITIES AND CIVIL NETWORKS

Title:

The Regenerative Sufficiency Charter for Cities and Civil Networks

An Open-Source Framework for Local Post-Scarcity Governance

Introduction: Why Start Local

While the goals of sufficiency and abundance are global in scale, their implementation often begins locally — in communities with the vision, networks, and urgency to act before states or supranational bodies catch up.

Cities are:

- Closer to people's daily realities
- More agile in policy experimentation
- Anchored by civil society, not just markets or militarism
- Already pioneering solutions in housing, food systems, participatory budgeting, and energy democracy

Yet most cities are constrained by:

- State-level preemption
- Revenue limits
- Overreliance on property taxes
- Lack of public ownership of essential services
- Inherited austerity-era governance structures

The Regenerative Sufficiency Charter offers a template for municipal transformation — allowing local governments, co-ops, and civil society federations to formally commit to a post-scarcity model of governance, rooted in rights, reciprocity, and regeneration.

Core Principles of the Charter

1. Material Sufficiency Is a Local Right
    - No resident shall go without food, housing, health care, or mobility due to economic exclusion.
2. The Commons Shall Be Protected, Expanded, and Democratically Managed
    - Land, water, energy, digital access, and ecological spaces belong to the community, not corporations.
3. Budgeting Shall Be Participatory and Justice-Oriented
    - Residents co-create the city's budget with transparency and sufficiency benchmarks.
4. Regeneration Is a Civic Duty
    - Cities must operate within ecological boundaries, restore degraded ecosystems, and prioritize planetary health in all policies.

5. Care Work Shall Be Valued and Resourced
    - Unpaid care labor shall be recognized as foundational economic activity, supported through public infrastructure and time equity.
6. Local Knowledge and Cultural Sovereignty Shall Guide Design
    - Indigenous traditions, cultural diversity, and neighborhood wisdoms are centered in decision-making.

Legal Framework: Model Articles of Governance
Article I: Declaration of Sufficiency Rights
The city recognizes the right of every resident to:

- Permanent, safe, and dignified housing
- Sufficient and culturally appropriate food
- Free-at-point-of-use health care and mental wellness services
- Unrestricted education and knowledge access
- Non-commercial digital and mobility infrastructure
- Time for care, rest, and creative flourishing

Article II: Municipal Commons Trust
The city shall establish a Commons Trust Authority, governed by elected and randomly selected residents, to:

- Identify and protect public assets as commons
- Manage them in the public interest
- Partner with local cooperatives and collectives
- Ban privatization of essential services

Article III: Participatory Budget and Policy Design

- 30% (or more) of the municipal discretionary budget is allocated through citizen deliberation and vote.
- Budgeting sessions are multilingual, compensated, and inclusive of marginalized populations.
- All municipal policies are subjected to a Sufficiency and Ecological Impact Review.

Article IV: Local Economic Transition

- Transition from extractive contracts to community wealth-building procurement strategies
- Phase-in of:
    - Municipal job guarantees for sufficiency sectors
    - Land banking and public land trusts
    - Circular economies and community currencies
    - Universal utility access regardless of income

Article V: Emergency Sufficiency Protocols
In crisis events, the city may:

- Requisition vacant housing for emergency shelter
- Use public kitchens and food stores to ensure meal provision
- Suspend utility disconnections and medical billing

- Invoke local mutual aid networks and disaster co-ops as public partners

Civic Implementation Tools
  A. *People's Assemblies*
  Quarterly gatherings where residents:

- Review progress on sufficiency indicators
- Propose and debate new projects
- Elect Commons Trust representatives

  B. *Neighborhood Sufficiency Councils*
  Block- or district-level bodies responsible for:

- Identifying unmet needs
- Facilitating mutual aid coordination
- Participating in urban design and land-use planning

  C. *Post-Scarcity Data Hubs*

- Real-time dashboards tracking:
  - Empty homes vs. unhoused persons
  - Surplus food vs. hunger zones
  - Carbon emissions vs. local drawdown
- All data is open-source and tied to policy triggers

  D. *Municipal Sufficiency Bonds*

- Democratically governed public bond initiatives to fund:
  - Food forests
  - Transit cooperatives

- Elder care centers
- Energy retrofits
- Public broadband

Case Studies and Adaptations in Practice

- Barcelona (Spain): Decidim digital democracy platform, care economy budget
- Jackson (Mississippi): Cooperation Jackson's solidarity economy ecosystem
- Preston (UK): Community wealth building through local procurement
- Seoul (South Korea): Social economy incubators and public housing unions
- Bogotá (Colombia): Care blocks, feminist budgeting, transit justice programs

Each offers blueprints for adapting the Charter to diverse political, cultural, and economic contexts.

Becoming a Regenerative City

Cities adopting the Charter may publicly affiliate with the International Coalition of Post-Scarcity Municipalities (ICPSM) — a voluntary network sharing:

- Best practices
- Participatory tools
- Policy prototypes
- Legal support for charter defense

Membership criteria include:

- Passing a local version of the Charter by vote or council
- Demonstrating progress on sufficiency metrics annually
- Engaging in at least one regional or global collaborative project

Final Note

The nation-state may be slow to move. But the neighborhood moves swiftly.

And when enough cities reclaim sufficiency, the world will follow.

This Charter is not merely policy. It is a promise to never again tolerate hunger amid abundance, or isolation in a city full of people.

DRAFTING TOMORROW – SAMPLE LOCAL CHARTER LANGUAGE, DRAFT CHARTER FOR COOPERATIVES, INTENTIONAL COMMUNITIES, AND NETWORKS OF PRACTICE

Sufficiency Rights Clause (Municipal Template):
"Every resident of [CITY NAME] has the right to sufficient housing, food, medical care, education, mobility, and ecological stability, without discrimination or precondition. The City commits to ensuring these rights through participatory governance, commons stewardship, and budgetary priority."

Commons Protection Language:
"The following resources shall be protected as community commons: public water, air quality, digital infrastructure, public lands, and knowledge systems. No sale, lease, or delegation of control shall occur without direct community consent."

Draft Charter
Title:
The Living Sufficiency Charter: A Framework for Post-Scarcity Practice in Civil Society

Introduction: When the People Govern Themselves
While cities can wield political and budgetary power,

many of the most powerful engines of transformation reside outside formal government — in kitchens, libraries, farms, cooperatives, collectives, spiritual circles, and organizing hubs where people co-create solutions long before policy catches up.

In these spaces, governance is lived.

The Living Sufficiency Charter offers a shared framework for aligning grassroots institutions with the values of:

- Material sufficiency
- Mutual care
- Ecological repair
- Democratic stewardship
- Decolonization
- Abundant belonging

It's not a blueprint, but a compass — adaptable across cultures, geographies, and political realities, yet rooted in one core truth:

The commons lives wherever people share what they need, without exploitation or exclusion.

Core Principles of the Charter

1. Need Before Profit
    - Collective provisioning exists to meet needs, not maximize revenue or prestige.
2. Shared Stewardship
    - Resources are held in common, managed democratically, and passed to future generations in better condition.
3. Interdependence

- The health of any member is the concern of all. Care, rest, and reciprocity are structured, not assumed.
4. Radical Transparency
    - Budgets, decisions, and impacts are visible and accountable to all participants.
5. Ecological Boundaries
    - Production and consumption must not exceed regenerative capacity. Nature is not a raw material — it is a member.
6. Reparative Commitment
    - Active efforts to redress historical injustices — racial, colonial, gendered, ecological — are baked into structures, not outsourced to values statements.

Operational Framework: Articles of Practice
Article I: Commitment to Sufficiency
Each member of the collective agrees to:

- Contribute according to ability
- Receive according to need
- Ensure that no member experiences hunger, homelessness, medical abandonment, or social exclusion

Article II: Governance Structure

- All members hold equal voice and vote, with adaptations for disability, caregiving, and linguistic access
- Major decisions (budgets, land use, provisioning changes) require:

- Participatory deliberation
- Restorative consensus (or 75% majority where consensus fails)
* Regular (monthly or seasonal) assemblies are required

Article III: Resource Commons
The following assets must be governed collectively:

* Land, housing, and shelter infrastructure
* Tools, machinery, and production equipment
* Surplus food, medicine, or essential supplies
* Shared digital platforms and databases
* Cultural materials, knowledge archives, and rituals of meaning

Article IV: Provisioning Mechanisms
Each chartered community shall:

* Develop a Sufficiency Inventory (What do we have? What do we need?)
* Operate a Commons Exchange Hub or internal mutual credit system
* Coordinate provisioning in:
  - Food security (gardens, meal shares, procurement)
  - Health and wellness (care circles, herbal/medical cooperatives)
  - Housing stability (co-housing, land trusts, rent-free units)
  - Transportation (car shares, bike libraries, accessibility vans)

- Tech and connectivity (community Wi-Fi, device lending)

Article V: Conflict and Repair

- Disagreements are addressed through:
  - Restorative circles
  - Mediation panels elected by members
  - Collective accountability rituals
- Expulsion is a last resort, never tied to productivity, status, or belief — only to sustained harm or refusal to engage in repair

Civic Interconnection and Federation

Federation Principle:

- No post-scarcity community stands alone.

Communities chartered under the Living Sufficiency framework are encouraged to:

- Join regional and thematic federations
- Share data, strategies, and surplus through open-source platforms
- Participate in global Commons Congresses, Care Summits, or Digital Assemblies of Practice

These federations do not control — they connect and coordinate, supporting:

- Collective bargaining with states
- Pooling of resources across bioregions

- Shared defense against privatization, eviction, and criminalization

Cultural and Spiritual Dimensions
Chartered communities may embed shared:

- Ceremonies of welcome, birth, union, death
- Practices of reflection, song, or silence
- Time-based rhythms: market-free days, care sabbaths, rest months
- Annual reviews of sufficiency and abundance

These are not rules, but rituals of belonging — reminding us we are not systems engineers alone, but humans in a web of life.

How to Adopt the Charter

1. Host a Community Assembly
2. Introduce the Charter principles. Invite feedback. Translate, adapt, and rewrite as needed.
3. Affirm Consent and Modifications
4. Ratify via consensus or vote. Include meaningful input from children, elders, and disabled members.
5. Publicly Commit
6. Publish your Charter. Share your governance model. Join federated directories if desired.
7. Review Annually
8. Hold a "Day of Enough" to assess well-being, sufficiency gaps, ecological limits, and justice commitments.

Final Note

This Charter is not prescriptive. It is a living agreement between people who choose to build a different world not by lobbying those in power, but by becoming the power that cares, shares, and repairs.

The revolution is not just televised.

It is planted, cooked, healed, housed, translated, and made sacred — together.

SUGGESTED READING AND RESEARCH BASE

- Peter Joseph, *The New Human Rights Movement*
- Kate Raworth, *Doughnut Economics*
- Amartya Sen & Martha Nussbaum, *Capability Approach*
- Raj Patel & Jason W. Moore, *A History of the World in Seven Cheap Things*
- Elinor Ostrom, *Governing the Commons*
- Adrienne Maree Brown, *Emergent Strategy*
- Jason Hickel, *Less Is More*
- Silvia Federici, *Re-Enchanting the World*
- UN Special Rapporteur Reports on Extreme Poverty and Human Rights

www.ingramcontent.com/pod-product-compliance
Lightning Source LLC
Chambersburg PA
CBHW020532030426
42337CB00013B/826